LINK JUICE
Understanding and Using Backlinks for Better Search Rankings

Mike Wood

Copyright © 2017 Mike Wood

All rights reserved.

ISBN:
ISBN-13: 978-1542580489
ISBN-10: 154258048X

CONTENTS

	Preface	i
1	What Are Backlinks	1
2	Types of Links	12
3	Anchor Text	23
4	LSI Keywords	37
5	Link Diversity	47
6	Link Wheels and Link Farms	55
7	Content First, Backlinks Second	70
8	Link Building Strategies	82
9	Wikipedia Backlinks	105
BONUS	Nail Your Guest Post Pitch	112
BONUS	50 Shades of SEO Advice	124

PREFACE

My goals with this book are many. I want to provide you with a basic overview of backlinks, why they are important, and how to obtain them. However, I also want to provide you with information that will help you rank higher in search results and not get penalized by Google.

When acquiring backlinks you need to know more than simply how to get a backlink. It is the additional methods I talk about herein that will take you from a basic understanding of SEO to someone who will consistently rank pages.

The word "backlinks" carries somewhat of a bad connotation. Black-hat marketers have ruined the SEO industry with their backlink methods which is also one of the reasons I put this book together. I want to let people know that there are legitimate ways to acquire backlinks without falling into the world of black-hat SEO.

SEO and link acquisition methods change from time to time and you are ultimately responsible for your actions. I am simply sharing my stories and opinions on what has worked for me and my clients. Any method or strategy you use is at your own risk and I am not responsible for the results.

If you enjoy the book, please let the world know about it and leave a review on Amazon. I am also open-minded and love learning from others.

If there is something in the book you don't agree with or think needs to be expanded, please email and let me know. Who knows? I may quote you in next year's revised copy. (contact@legalmorning.com)

1 - WHAT ARE BACKLINKS

Backlinks and link building. Two terms you will need to become familiar with if you want to have any type of successful SEO (search engine optimization) strategy. In fact, links are one of the top ranking signals that Google uses to determine where to rank a website. So what is a backlink?

"For search engines that crawl the vast metropolis of the web, links are the streets between pages," according to Moz.com, a leading SEO agency started by world-renowned SEO expert, Rand Fishkin. "Using sophisticated link analysis, the engines can discover how pages are related to each other and in what ways."

Quite simply, a backlink is a hyperlink that links "back" to a website from a specific text, referred to as "anchor text" (more on that later). In order to fully understand how backlinks work and why they are so important, we need to discuss ranking signals and search results.

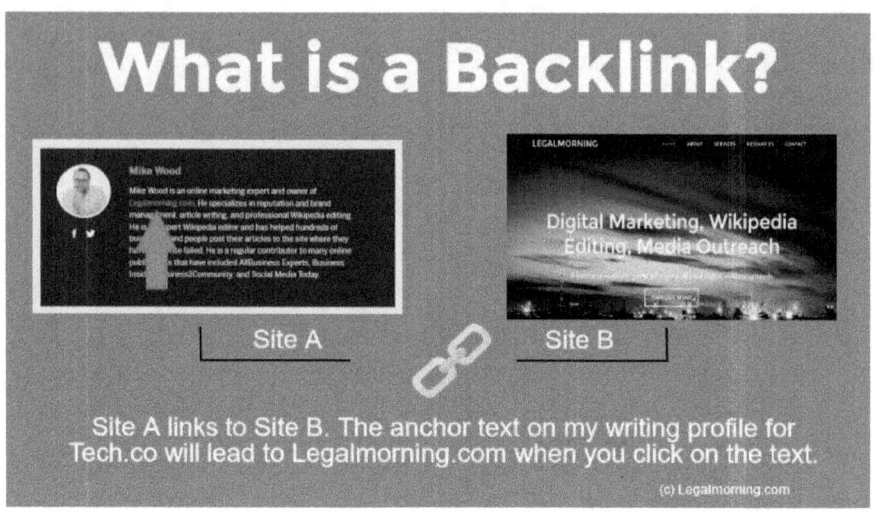

So, let's start off with a basic overview of how Google ranks its pages. Note that throughout this book I use "Google" quite a bit. Sometimes I am referring to Google, but often this can be applied to all search engines – Bing, Yahoo, DuckDuckGo, etc. Just note that Google gets the majority of search traffic which is why we focus on Google 99% of the time.

Ranking Signals and Search Results

Google has a daunting task. Whenever someone types in a search term, it goes on a quest through the entire internet looking for the websites that best fit that term. Search engine companies such as Yahoo! used to do this manually, but thanks to technology it is now done through algorithms.

Google has algorithms that are designed to find and return the best search results. When a term is entered into search, they take many things into consideration to determine which site gets the #1 spot and which sites don't even get ranked. These algorithms are updated on a regular basis, but there are certain ranking signals that have always stayed true through every update.

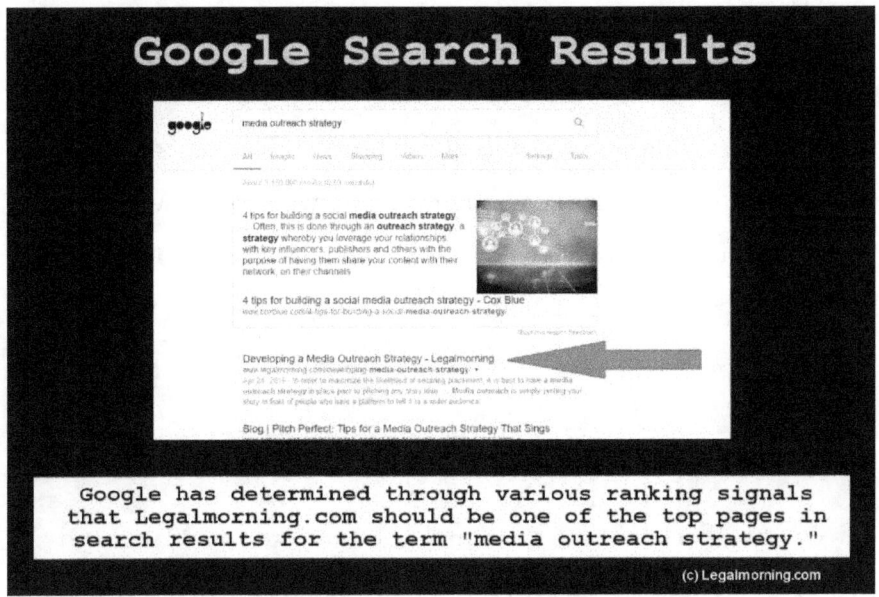

Ranking signals are indicators seen by the algorithm to let Google know your website should be ranked for specific keywords. One of the top ranking signals is backlinks. How do we know? Google told us.

"Of course, Google looks at many other factors, such as those on our *Periodic Table Of Ranking Factors*," writes Barry Schwartz, an SEO expert and News Editor for Search Engine Land. "Links, Content and RankBrain themselves; each are made up of many subfactors. But, these are the overall top three, officially confirmed by Google itself."

Google sees the backlinks coming to your website and uses them to help determine your ranking. Basically, Google believes if enough people are linking to your content, you must have good information to share.

Since this book is about backlinks, I will not dive much deeper into Google and how each of its algorithms work. That could be a book all in itself. Search Engine Land and various other websites have great guides that give you a basic overview of each. I would suggest you read up on each one and be familiar with any update that is released as it's important to your SEO strategy.

Understanding Backlink Value

No two backlinks are the same. They are like snowflakes and each one is unique in the eyes of Google. Years ago, backlinking was all about the numbers. The more backlinks you were able to acquire, the higher in search results you were likely to appear.

Google got smart, as they always do when someone comes along with another attempt to beat its ranking system. Through the years it has developed a way to value links from others. It uses the value of these links to determine the quality of your site and as a ranking factor to decide where to place you in search results. AJ Kumar says it the best in a piece he wrote for Entrepreneur.com.

"Since search engines can't manually assess the quality of every site, they rely on the number of backlinks pointing at a site and the relative quality of the links to determine a site's overall value," writes Kumar.

He also writes about link characteristics and link value. "There are backlink characteristics that matter in rankings algorithms. For example, a backlink from a high-ranked site will count more than one from a low-ranked site. A link from a relevant site within your industry also will get more weight."

So, a backlink from a website such as Entrepreneur.com will have a higher "link value" than a backlink from a new blog on a free platform such as Blogger.com. Why? Think about it. Google knows that Entrepreneur is likely only linking to authoritative information. The other blog? Not so much.

You will hear many times when learning about SEO that Google wants "quality," not "quantity." This is true for content as well as backlinks. It wants to see links coming to your site from trusted sources.

While there is no publicly known formula for accurately determining a link's value, here are some things that will help you understand which links will have more weight.

Domain Authority – Domain authority (DA) is a ranking given by Moz.com to determine the ranking authority of a site in Google.

Basically, a website with a higher DA is more likely to be ranked higher than a website with a lower DA for the same term. Many SEOs believe that getting links from high DA websites is the best thing you can do for link building. While having links from high DA is a good thing, you will also need to keep in mind link diversity (more on that a few chapters from now).

Follow / No-Follow – Some links are considered "no-follow" which means that Google will not take them into consideration when it comes to ranking. As such, no-follow links "technically" have no value at all (see chapter on link diversity).

Site Popularity – This includes domain authority described above, but you also need to consider overall site traffic. I use Alexa.com to determine site popularity. It ranks each website based on incoming traffic over a three month period. So, while a website may currently have a low DA (or high DA), its recent traffic will give you an idea on where the site is going in the near future (higher or lower). The more popular the site, the higher the value of the link.

Link Farms – We will talk more about link farms later, but basically they are sites set up by SEO professionals for the sole purpose of generating backlinks. Links coming from these sites can have a harmful effect on your website.

Reciprocal / Paid Links – If you are exchanging links or paying for links, Google will be able to tell. Any link that is reciprocal or paid will have value, but not a good value. Google will actually consider it spam and likely penalize your site and remove it from search results altogether.

Trusted Websites – Links from trusted websites will be valued more by Google. A trusted website is one that will have high traffic, high domain authority, and plenty of backlinks to it from other trusted sites. A great tool to determine trust is from Majestic who assigned a trust-flow score for each backlink to your website.

I could go on for a few more pages with various link value considerations, but I think that horse is dead and buried. Logic should take over at this point and you can determine which websites will give you more backlink value than others.

Keep link value in mind when you begin link acquisition. There will be many SEO providers that guarantee you "X" number of links for a specific amount of money. Remember, it is about quality and not quantity. A link acquired from a high-quality source will do you more good than 10 links from sources that aren't.

Why Use Backlinks?

You can already see why it is important to use backlinks. Since Google uses them as a factor in ranking your website, you would be wise to have a backlink acquisition strategy. But, are there other reasons why you should want backlinks?

Absolutely, and this is one most people miss. Links were originally created to lead people to additional information about a topic. Over the years, so much focus has gone into using them for SEO that many forget about their original intended purpose – to BRING TRAFFIC to your website.

We will talk about this a little later, but links need to lead to quality content. If not, Google will de-value the link and you will get little (if any) SEO value. So, it is important to acquire links to quality content on your website. In addition to the SEO value, readers who come to your website are leads that you have a chance to convert. Give them crappy content to read, they will leave and go to your competitor.

Black-Hat Techniques

I touched briefly on the fact that some people have attempted to trick Google into ranking them higher in the search results. And some still do try. They use various methods to manipulate ranking, all of which are referred to as "black-hat" methods or techniques.

I want to bring some of these techniques to your attention as you will likely run into people using these methods – normally the ones who tell you they can get you ranked #1 in Google. They are right in that they can rank you high in Google, but that will only last a short time before Google detects the manipulation and drops you from results completely. The fact is, a reputable SEO firm will never offer you guaranteed search results.

5 Reasons Why Reputable SEO Firms Don't Provide Guaranteed Search Engine Rankings

According to Rand Fishkin from Moz

#1 SEO & Guarantees Have an Abominable History (SEOs providing too-good-to-be-true promises with guarantees have tainted the use of the word "guarantee."

#2 The Search Engines Expressly Warn Against It

#3 Rankings are Inherently Unstable

#4 Rankings are a Poor Metric for Overall Performance

#5 Making Guarantees About Something You Cannot Control Carries Inherent Ethical Problems

(c) Legalmorning.com

Information Source - https://moz.com/blog/why-reputable-seo-firms-dont-promise-guaranteed-search-engine-rankings

Engaging in black-hat tactics is very attractive as the thought of ranking high quickly is very appealing. However, you can also rank quickly through proper link acquisition techniques that I cover later in this book. Do not fall for the "rank quick" schemes as you will only be penalized by Google and sent back to the back of the class, having to start from the beginning of trying to rank again.

Some of the black-hat methods previously used include generating as many backlinks to a website as possible. As discussed, Google does not take the total number of a links as a sole ranking factor. The quality of links is now important and a website can rank high for few backlinks if they are of high quality. Make sure all of your links have good link value as previously discussed.

Link wheels and link farms will be discussed later in the book as well. Link wheels are good if done properly, but most are not. They simply link to you from websites set up for the sole purpose of generating links. Google knows who these sites are and you don't want to be related to them once penalties get handed out. Guilt by association happens quite frequently when Google penalizes a link farm.

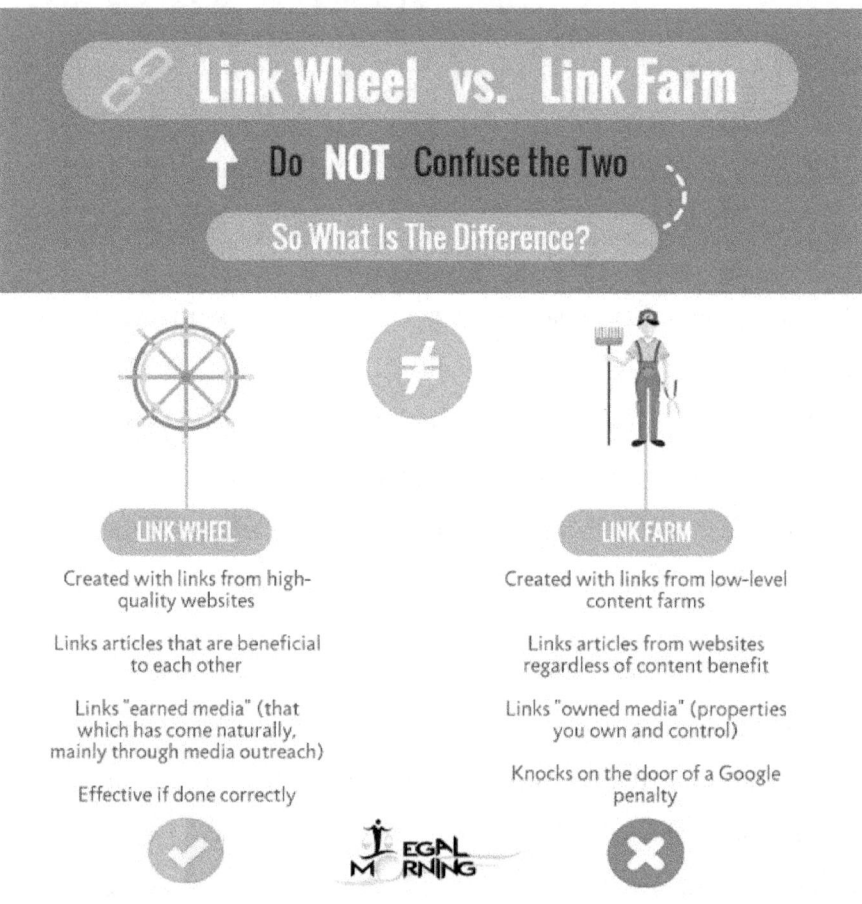

There are dozens more black-hat techniques that I could cover here, but I am going to focus more on the proper way to acquire links. And don't just take it from me, black-hat SEO techniques, including those used for acquiring backlinks, no longer work.

"Today, nearly all black-hat techniques no longer work," writes Eric Wendt, writer and editor for content marketing agency Brafton.com. "What's more, employing them can do serious harm to your placement on search engine results pages. This makes it more important than ever to parse good from bad when it comes to SEO."

Just keep in mind that if something sounds too good to be true, it probably is. I highly recommend that you learn as much as you can about any link building technique you want to use. However, if it is in any way associated with the term black-hat, run like hell.

I even recommend researching the strategies I teach you in this book. The "trust but verify" concept is strong when it comes to any SEO technique.

2 - TYPES OF LINKS

Now that you know what a backlink is, its purpose, and some ways to determine each one's value, let's take a look at a few types of backlinks. It is important to understand each type in order to ensure proper backlink distribution. You will need to know them for the purpose of link diversity and anchor text.

Don't think I am going to make things too complicated here. This chapter is basically for you to understand the terminology associated with backlinking. The reason you want to understand the various types is because of link diversity.

Do-Follow Versus No-Follow Links

Link attributes are often a topic of discussion when it comes to link acquisition. When we talk about "do-follow" (sometimes referred to simply as "follow") and "no-follow" attributes, we are talking Google. Does Google "follow" this link, or not, for the purpose of ranking?

Google sees each backlink coming into your website and takes them into consideration for ranking. When a link is no-follow, it is telling Google not to count it or "follow" it when considering rank.

"Nofollow provides a way for webmasters to tell search engines, "Don't follow links on this page" or "Don't follow this specific link."" – Google.

People who engage in link acquisition chase the do-follow link as if it is the Holy Grail. After all, why obtain a link that Google will not take into consideration for ranking? What I like to ask people is if no-follow links don't matter, why do so many people want a backlink from Wikipedia (a backlink that has a no-follow attribute)? Again, you will appreciate this more when we get into link diversity a little later.

So why would a link ever be no-follow? Well, remember that backlinks are used for more than just ranking purposes. You want to lead people to valuable information. That goal is accomplished regardless of the attributes assigned to it.

Some people assign a no-follow attribute to a link because of its potential for being spammy. If someone does not trust a link (then they shouldn't be using the link in the first place but you can only lead the horse to water), a webmaster may assign this attribute so as not to get penalized by Google.

Google also recommends assigning no-follow attributes to certain links that webmasters may be concerned about. These can include affiliate links.

"In most cases, Google handles affiliate links without any issue, as they know about the majority of affiliate networks," writes Harsh Agrawal, discussing a recommendation on affiliate links made by former head of Google's spam team, Matt Cutts. "But if you are still worried, you can add a no-follow link to such money links."

Adding a no-follow attribute allows you to still receive any financial benefit from the link without worrying that Google will penalize you for it.

There are a number of ways to tell if a backlink is follow or no-follow. Here are two of the most common.

- **Source Code** – Right-click on the web page where the backlink originates from. Click on "view page source" and review the HTML code. Simply search for the term "nofollow." If it takes you to the wording and it is placed in the link code, you have found a no-follow link. You will need a basic understanding of HTML to be able to do this.

- **Browser Extension** – You can install a browser extension or add-on which will give you a visual indication of no-follow links. I use one for Firefox that highlights all no-follow links in pink. I can easily see which links are do-follow and which ones are no-follow without the need to look at any source code.

Do-follow and no-follow links will likely be the first topic of discussion for any link you are trying to acquire. As I will discuss later, do not be scared to acquire no-follow links as you will actually want to add a percentage of them to your link profile during your acquisition strategy.

Affiliate Links

I just touched on affiliate links above but want to cover them a little more in-depth. Affiliate links are a great source of potential revenue for your website so you will want to use them if applicable. However, they can cause an ugly looking link profile for your website and potentially get you penalized if not done correctly.

As stated, an affiliate link is one that leads to a website where you can earn income for that referral. Here is how it works.

Let's say you own a website about book reviews. As you are writing about books, it is only natural to link to the actual book in case people want to buy it. As an affiliate marketer you can earn commission for each book sold when you make that referral (such as through Amazon Associates, a referral program from Amazon.com). Another great example are websites such as Ebates which get paid a certain percentage of all sales generated from websites they refer people to.

Affiliate links have specific codes so that a website knows you are the one making a referral. The website then tracks sales, leads, or whatever it is you are going to be compensated for. If you can't already see the problem here, let me make it a little clearer.

When you use a link for the purpose of generating revenue, Google can see this as spam. After all, Google wants you to use links to inform readers, not line your pockets. Affiliate links can be tricky to deal with, so many webmasters, such as myself, no-follow any referral links.

Contextual / Widget / Header / Footer / Sidebar

Okay, that's really like five different kinds of links (math isn't my strong point). I cover them all together because they are all related to each other. For these five sets of links, it all depends on the location where the link is on a website.

Contextual links are the most common form of link you think of when it comes to backlinks. These are the links in the body of a page or article. They are part of the content that people read and hyperlink to other information outside the content.

The rest are pretty self-explanatory. Widget links are links inside of widgets, footer links are the links in the footer of a web page, etc. When engaging in link acquisition, contextual links are by far the ones you want to get. Neil Patel, one of the leading authorities of

SEO agrees:

"Google's algorithm does not count backlinks equally," writes Patel. "Links in the footer, sidebar and navigation don't carry much weight."

Internal, External, and Backlinks

Links can also be classified based on where they lead. A backlink is one that comes to your website from another. An internal link is one that links to other content in your website. An external link is one that leads from your website to another website.

Here's a brain teaser for you. Imagine a link leading from "Website A" to "Website B." It will be considered a backlink by B, but an external link by A. Don't worry, that's about as Einsteiny as I get.

Internal links are extremely important when it comes to having an effective backlink strategy. You want to show Google that not only do other people want to link to you, but that you want to link to it as well. It can also have a direct impact on your ranking.

"Your site architecture – the way you structure and organize internal links (e.g., a link to the About Us section of your website from your main navigation) – plays a vital role in how both users and search engines are able to navigate your website, ultimately impacting your website's rankings." – Paul Shapiro, Search Engine Land

Make sure that content on your website is linked to other relevant content on your website. Internal links are another ranking factor for SEO purposes and if you have none, then don't expect to receive any benefit.

External backlinks are also important as you are not the ultimate authority on everything. You need to link to relevant information from high-quality websites. When Google sees this, they will know you have good content as you received it from quality sources.

"I'm here to tell you that using external links on your website is not only perfectly fine, it is both directly and indirectly good for your SEO efforts because ultimately, it serves the user – your customer." – Marcus Maraih, Standard Marketing.

Of course, this book is about backlinks so enough about internal and external. Just want you to get the terms down for when you're at your next marketing get-together and others start throwing about the lingo.

Natural (Editorial) and Unnatural Links

* Sigh * The term "natural" link is something that gets thrown away way too often by SEO professionals and many of them do not understand the true definition. When I hear it, I just roll my eyes and move on. When you hear the term natural, it is referring to a link that naturally occurs without any effort of your own (this is also referred to as an "editorial" link).

What? Okay, let me explain further. Technically, all "link building" is against Google best practices because Google does not believe you should have to build your own backlinks. Google expects people to link to you "naturally" meaning they happened to come across your website, found your content interesting, and decided to link to it because it was the best thing since sliced bread.

Okay. That seems logical, but how do people find you? We know that people rarely go to page two of the search results. That means only 10 websites are likely to receive the backlinks out of the one billion currently live on the World Wide Web. So how do they find you again? Through link acquisition methods.

The takeaway from this is not to get too caught up in the terminology – natural and unnatural. What Google does not consider natural is often fine and what some consider unnatural would actually not violate Google's linking guidelines. Here is how I like to think of it.

Any link that you pay for, exchange, or otherwise acquire through influence is unnatural. Any link you acquire because someone decides your content is of quality to do so, regardless if they scrolled through one billion web pages or you sent them an outreach email, would be considered natural. Some SEOs actually agree with how I look at natural and unnatural links.

"Natural links are links created in the process of you "doing what you do" online," writes Rune Jensen in an article on acquiring natural backlinks, published on Rank Scanner in 2015. "This has also earned them the nickname "organic links". They are not the links you oh-so-carefully attempt to shove into unrelated content, links you pay for, links you sell and other manufactured attempts to increase your own site's web traffic, and not maintaining a genuine focus on customer acquisition efforts."

Okay, okay, Rune. We are now on the same page.

Text / Video / Image Links

Normally we think of links as the blue underlined text within a sentence. This is considered a text link and is the most common. However, there are two additional links that you need to know about.

Image links are very popular. These are the type that lead to another website when you click on them. These are most common with call to action buttons. An example is on Amazon.com when you see the button "add to cart." It is an image (sometimes called a button link) that leads to another location or tells the website to take another action.

Video links are a little more complicated but are being used more and more. When you watch a video on YouTube, you will see ads that pop up or play before your regular video. By clicking on the video, you will be taken to the location being advertised. This is sort of an image link but can change as the video plays (the link location will differ depending on the ad that is playing).

Reciprocal Links

Reciprocal links are those that link between two properties. The link from website "A" links to website "B" and vice versa. These links are not a good idea as it appears similar to a link exchange which Google sees as a black-hat method of building links. Reciprocal links are normally made when two webmasters agree to exchange links which is why it is not a good idea to engage in the practice.

Blog Comment Links

Blog comment links are hyperlinks made from information you enter when making a comment on a blog post. When you make a comment on a WordPress blog, you are asked for three pieces of information – your name, your website address, and the actual comment. After you enter the comment, WordPress creates a hyperlink with your name that leads to the website address you entered.

Note that I am not referring to links within the text of a comment, which would be considered text links (bare URLs or links with anchor text). These are very spammy. I suggest never placing a link into the text of a blog comment unless you are looking for traffic and not page rank.

Signature Links

Signature links are literally links in your signature. These are mainly used in forums so that any time you sign off a comment it will lead to a certain location. Pretty easy huh?

3 - ANCHOR TEXT

Now let's talk about anchor text: One of the most useful, yet abused, ranking signals when it comes to SEO. Many people fail to understand how to properly use anchor text and then get frustrated when they are penalized or their content doesn't rank.

Anchor text is the most important thing to know when acquiring backlinks. Understand what it is, how to properly use it, mix in link diversity, and you have a recipe for ranking content for specific keywords.

What is Anchor Text?

Anchor text is simply the wording used to link to another page or website. It is normally highlighted in blue and gives the reader an indication of what they are linking to. For instance, when you link from the term "what is anchor text," you expect that it leads to another page that discusses anchor text.

How Anchor Text Affects SEO

As stated above, anchor text indicates what you are linking to. When it comes to SEO, Google sees the anchor text and decides how relevant that page is to the topic. Using the example above, Google will try to determine how relevant a specific page is that is linked from the anchor text "what is anchor text."

Once Google determines its relevancy, it will rank that page in search results for that anchor text. So, you can see the benefit of using anchor text that matches the keyword you want to rank for. However, you can probably already see the potential for abuse as well.

In the early days of search, Google relied too heavily on anchor text. It focused almost exclusively on anchor text as a ranking signal. So, the more links you had from the anchor text "what is anchor text," the higher you ranked for that term. SEOs figured this out quickly and began manipulating search results by building backlinks from exact match anchor text.

When Google founders were still partying at Stanford, they wrote a paper which presented the idea of a large-scale search engine (what eventually became Google) that relied on hyperlinks.

"The text of links is treated in a special way in our search engine," wrote Google founders, Sergey Brin and Larry Page, back in the day. "Most search engines associate the text of a link with the page that the link is on. In addition, we associate it with the page the link points to."

(On a side note, the paper referenced above only spent four paragraphs on the potential of Google's scalability. If only Brin and Page knew then what they know now, they could have gone to class in their self-driving cars, using navigation mapped out by their own satellites while traveling through urban infrastructures designed with their technology. And if they are late, they can send a Gmail using their Pixel phones which will ultimately be delivered to their professor via Google Fiber ... [deep breath]).

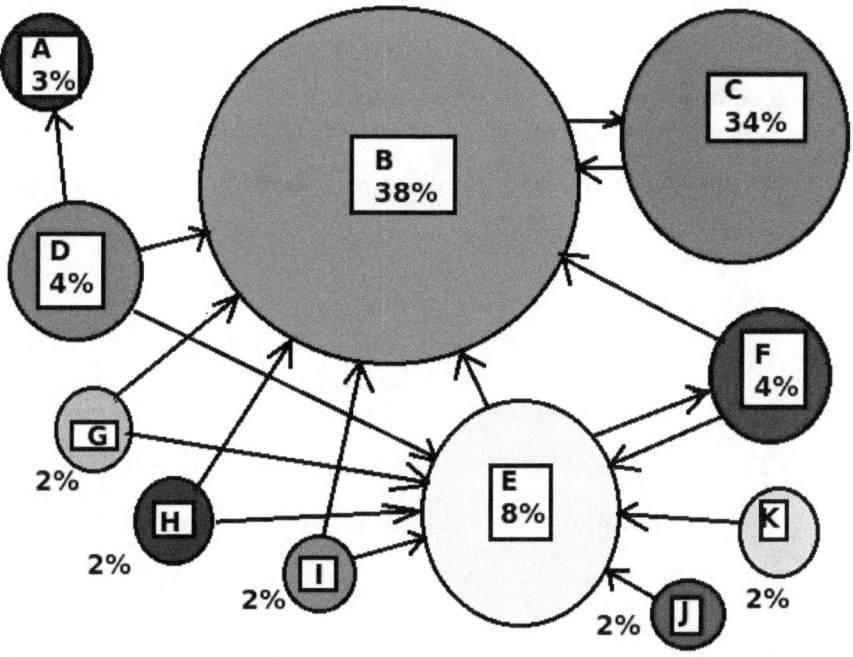

Here is how heavily Google used to rely on anchor text. Since website B is the recipient of numerous inbound links, it ranked more highly in a web search. And the links "carry through", such that website C, even though it only had one inbound link, had an inbound link from a highly popular site, website B. (Note: percentages are rounded. Modified text and image courtesy of Wikimedia Commons.)

It was similar to an arms race, yet with backlinks. Webmasters and SEOs began building links at a furious pace and diluted the quality of information available on the internet. Google eventually caught up and punished websites for doing so which is why I preach link diversity.

Brin and Page gave away part of their secret sauce in the early days and it was abused heavily. This is exactly why Google does not disclose how its algorithms work now. It keeps marketers honest.

However, anchor text is still a strong ranking signal. But, before you go out and build links for the exact same anchor text, please read on.

Types of Anchor Text

There are numerous types of anchor text. You need to know them all when acquiring backlinks as it will help keep you from getting coal from Google this Christmas.

When we get into link diversity, you will see how important it is to use different types of anchor text. For now, I will simply show you some of the most commonly known and used for backlinks.

Exact Match Anchor Text

According to WordStream, "an exact match anchor text has the same keywords highlighted as the targeted keyword of a web page." So what does this mean? If you want to rank a page for the keyword "Christmas trees," using the term "Christmas trees" as the anchor text leading to that page, this would be considered an exact match anchor text.

Exact match anchor text is beneficial for trying to rank specific terms, but it can also be a liability thanks to Google Penguin, an algorithm update released by Google in 2012 that began penalizing people for overuse of exact-match. It was meant to target those who were using exact match anchor text to manipulate search results.

"Remember, manipulating search engine rankings is not what search engines want," writes Kaila Strong, talking about the Google Penguin release. "With the recent Penguin update Google identified this tactic as invalid. They did this by examining the **percentage of exact match anchor text to websites as an entire domain** [emphasis added], and as individual pages as well. One clear way of identifying a site that has tried to manufacture links or manipulate search engine rankings is anchor text."

Branded Anchor Text

Branded anchor text is when you link from the name of a website. For instance, you link the term "Legalmorning" to the website "http://www.legalmorning.com." This is one of the most common text anchors when someone is referencing a company by name.

"Branded anchors are the safest type of anchor text if you have a branded domain," says Nathan Gotch of Gotch SEO (see what I did there with the link?).

Referring Domains Count	Referring Domains with Anchor	Referring Pages Count	Referring Pages with Anchor	Anchor Text
1. 11,336	50%	271,125	41%	best buy
2. 3,233	14%	20,683	3%	www.bestbuy.com
3. 1,437	6%	10,828	2%	http://www.bestbuy.com
4. 1,366	6%	56,293	9%	bestbuy.com
5. 1,288	6%	98,887	15%	bestbuy
6. 1,065	5%	3,741	0.57%	http://www.bestbuy.com/
7. 849	4%	84,446	13%	<a>noText</a>

In an article about various types of anchor text, Gotch provides an example for Best Buy. The graph shows that Best Buy has over 11,000 links from the anchor text "best buy", accounting for 41% of all incoming links.

Branded + Exact Match Anchors

So, let's combine two anchor text types we already discussed. This is a good way to let Google and readers know exactly "who" and "what" you are linking to before the link is ever clicked. Here is an example of how I would use this type of anchor text to link to an eBook:

"link building guide from Legalmorning"

"Legalmorning's guide to link building"

In order for this to be considered a branded + exact match, it MUST link to the domain you refer to in the link. Using the example above, the link must lead to my website Legalmorning and NOT to another website such as Amazon.com.

I recommend, as with exact match anchors, that you do not abuse this. Treat it as an exact match anchor and don't oversaturate your link profile with it. Simply use it to complement your existing branded and exact match anchors you are already trying to rank for. Here, you are just combining both into one.

Generic Anchor Text

Want to know more about generic anchors? **Click here!** Yes, I like to try to be funny (although my wife says otherwise). If you didn't get the joke, just move on.

Generic anchor text includes terms such as "click here," "find out more," or "go here." These are safe to keep you out of running into trouble with exact match anchors, but it does very little for ranking signals. According to Google, the anchor text you use should provide at least a basic idea of what you are linking to.

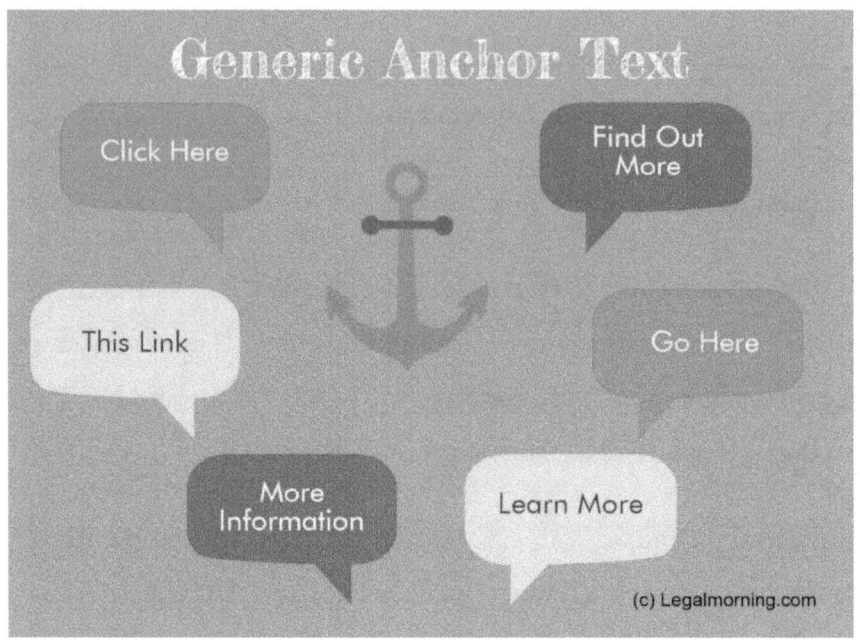

So why would someone ever use generic anchors if it doesn't provide that much (if any) benefit? Again, link diversity, link diversity, and link diversity. I also almost forgot … link diversity. In an article on MOZ discussing alternatives to generic links, Cyrus Shepard writes the following:

"After Google rolled out their Penguin update and over-optimization penalties in 2012, many SEOs discovered that too much exact-match anchor text was now a bad thing. Research suggests that successful backlink profiles actually contained a wide variety of anchor text including exact match, partial match, URL links, and even nofollow links."

So, generic anchor text is good for link diversity, but you need to make sure to let Google have a hint about what you are linking to. I would advise to make the anchor part of a whole sentence such as this:

"To find out more about link diversity check out my [guide] on anchor text."

Or

"[Download] my latest guide on link diversity and anchor text variations."

Naked Anchor Text

Naked anchor text, sometimes call a "bare URL", is about as basic as you can get. For naked anchor text, your anchor is the actual URL. For example, I can link the term "Legalmorning.com" to the homepage for Legalmorning.com. Don't get this confused with branded anchor text, though.

A great example is The Home Depot. If you link to the website homepage from the anchor text "The Home Depot," you are using a branded anchor text. If you link from the term "Homedepot.com," you are using naked anchor text.

Think of it like this. Branded is linking from the company name while naked is linking from a variation of the website URL. You will sometimes find these at the end of articles cited as sources instead of using anchor text within the body. A well-known website that does this is Natural News. You can read the content of an article that does not contain anchor text in the body, yet still see the sources they cite at the end of the page.

Partial Match Anchor Text

Partial match anchor text is when you use the keyword you want in conjunction with other descriptive text. This is also a common technique for using keywords when writing your landing page content as it will help rank for the keyword while avoiding "keyword stuffing."

Here is an example of partial match anchor text for the exact match text "jelly donut."

"**jelly donut**s"

"strawberry **jelly donut**"

"**jelly donut** bakery"

Partial match anchor text are some of my favorite. It tells your readers and Google what the page is about. However, it does not overuse exact match anchor, ultimately staying clear of any punishment from Penguin.

Using partial match anchor also gives you a broader keyword pattern for ranking. This means you will not only rank for "jelly donut," but the variations of the term. Again, Cyrus Shepard from Moz will enlighten us about partial match anchor text:

"Statistically though, this is your best choice. This is going to contain some of your exact matches, but you're going to have such a bigger broad tail, long tail queries that you can rank for. You're going to get more traffic. You're going to rank better for your targeted keywords, and this method is future proof. As Google de-emphasizes these exact matches, this is going to take you forward in the long run. Those links are going to have a lot longer long-term value, and it is just going to give you a better natural-looking link profile."

Long-Tail Anchor Text

Long-tail anchor text is similar to partial match anchor text. The only difference is that the anchor is long as hell (hence the term obviously – I am not sure why the name "long ass anchor text" got vetoed, but oh well). The easiest way to explain this is to just show you.

Let's use the example above for "jelly donut." You will use that exact phrase by incorporating it into partial match anchor text. Then, you will simply add to that.

"jelly donut with grape jelly"
"the last time I will eat a jelly donut in public"
"why we call them jelly donuts"

There are benefits for using long-tail anchor text. Since people like to ask questions, you can do an "exact match" for that question. For instance, maybe you decide to use the long-tail phrase "best type of jelly donut for gaining weight." This would help you rank high when people ask the question – "what are the best types of jelly donuts for gaining weight?"

Now, overuse of long-tail anchor text can be bad. For one, it can often be too broad for Google to know what you are talking about. For instance, Google may think the link for "best type of jelly donut for gaining weight" leads to a page on "foods that make you gain weight" or possibly "dangers of eating jelly donuts." Remember, Google is smart, but it isn't human. As such, I recommend matching your variations as closely as possible. For example:

"jelly donuts and weight gain"

"jelly donuts cause weight gain"

"gain weight eating jelly donuts"

Despite the potential for Google to confuse the rank signal from this type of anchor, you must still use it. Why? Well, 56 percent of buyers who search use queries of three or more words, while only 7 percent use one word of an acronym, according to WordStream. You will need to send some type of ranking signal showing Google your content is relevant to those 3+ word searches people are now using.

Make Sure to Vary Your Anchor Text

I will discuss link diversity later in the book, but wanted to touch on it briefly here. Part of link diversity involves varying your anchor text. You can see that using the exact same anchor text over and over will likely lead to a drop in search (even if it leads to a temporary increase).

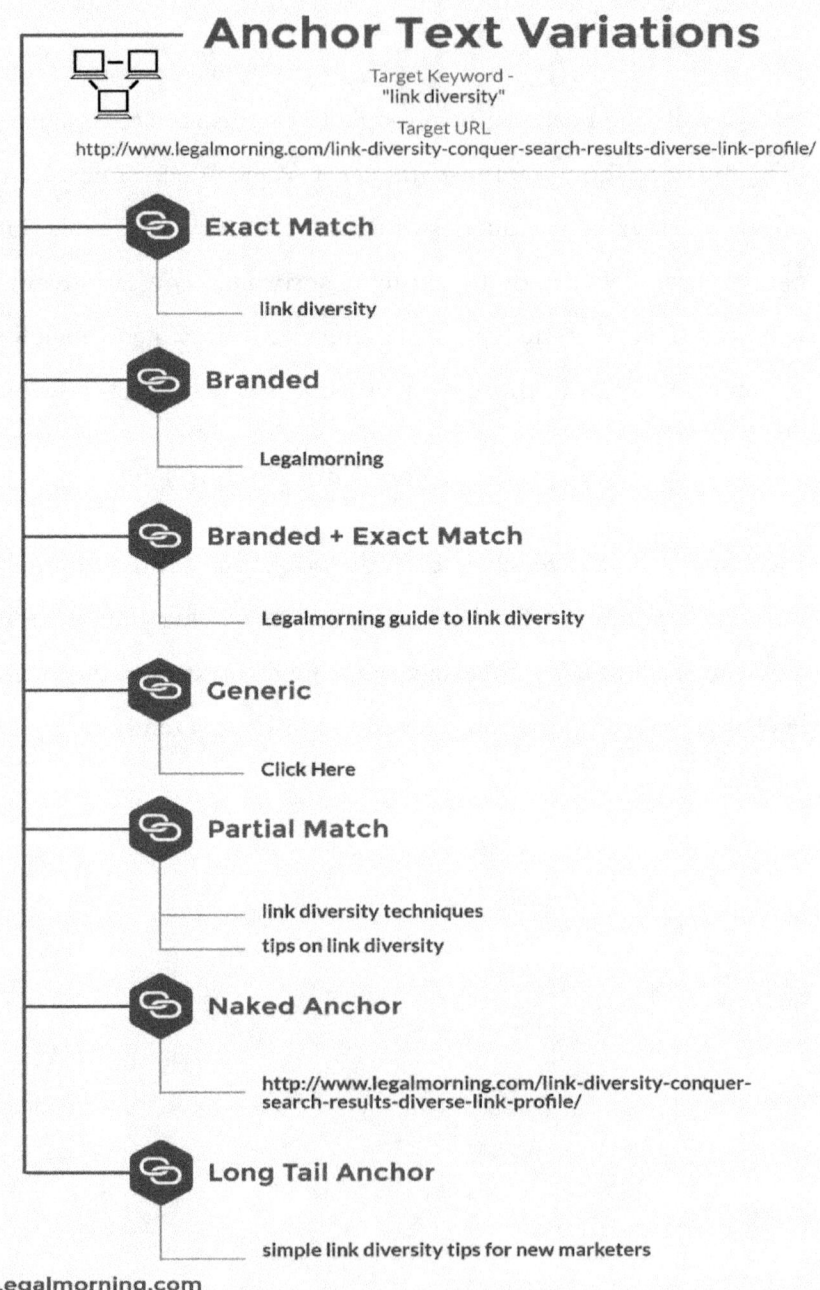

4 - LSI KEYWORD ANCHOR TEXT

Using LSI keywords is more of an on-site optimization technique than a backlink technique. So why in the hell would I waste your time talking about them? Great question – but I have an even better answer.

I have already covered anchor text previously in this book, but I wanted to cover this separately as I believe it to be one of the best ways to achieve link diversity in your anchor text. Not only does it vary the anchor text you use, but it also keeps the variations relevant to the terms you want to rank for.

You can skip to the end of this chapter if you want the short version, but I recommend reading it in its entirety. Once you understand LSI keywords and how they affect SEO, you will have a leg up on others when choosing anchor text for your backlinks.

What Are LSI Keywords?

LSI keywords are something that many use, but often do not know they are doing it. LSI is short for "latent semantic indexing," a term used to describe how search engines relate similar words or phrases to return search results.

According to *Beginners Book*, "latent semantic indexing keywords (or LSI keywords) are nothing but SEO terms for related keywords or synonyms."

LSI keywords are foreign to most. For those that are familiar with the term, very few understand how these words and phrases can help in your search rankings.

In 1999, Thomas Hofmann did a great paper for UC Berkeley titled "probabilistic latent semantic indexing" on the science behind LSI. If you want to know the technical details, you can read the paper. However, since we are marketers and not scientists, the only thing we really need to know is the simple definition and how it applies to SEO.

Quite simply, LSI is the use of similar words or word groups that identify the search term you are trying to find.

How Do LSI Keywords Affect Search?

Let's say you want to search for "affordable SEO." When you begin to type the term into Google, you will see suggestions that auto-fill in the search box. One such suggested search would be for "affordable SEO services." Because of LSI, Google knows that people searching for the term "affordable SEO" will likely want results relating to "affordable SEO services" as well.

Even if you choose your actual search term and not the suggested search term, Google will still return results for the other based on LSI. From the summary of each search result for "affordable SEO," you can see variations of the keyword – including "affordable SEO services," "affordable SEO prices," and "cheap SEO services."

Google has determined these phrases to be very similar in nature and as such returned articles containing these words. In the example above, your main keyword phrase is "affordable SEO" (the term you search for), and the other keyword phrases are LSI keywords (what Google has determined you want to know).

When it comes to on-site optimization, I always recommend using LSI keywords. When you create an article for a specific search term, find LSI keywords for the term you want to rank for. Include the LSI keywords in the article as well and you will start to rank for all the associated terms.

Using LSI keywords also helps your quality score according to Business2Community. "Search engines check for LSI keywords while indexing the content of a website. Specifically, they use these keywords as a measuring stick to determine the quality of content, so content that includes primary keywords in moderation and its LSI variations has the best chances of ranking high in search engines."

How to Find LSI Keywords

The next couple of paragraphs will talk about how to manually find LSI keywords. However, save yourself some time and simply find an online property that offers the service for free. I like to use the website LSIGraph.com as it seems to return exactly what I can find manually. Only difference? It gives me results in a matter of seconds.

Despite having the ability to do this through an LSI keyword generator as stated above, you should actually try to do this manually so you get a better feel for it. One of the easiest ways to do this manually is to simply type your search term in Google and hit enter.

Google will return plenty of results, but at the bottom of the page you will see a heading of "searches related to." There will by hyperlinks to additional keyword phrases that Google feels you also may want to search for. Guess what? These are your LSI keywords.

Another method is to look at the summary of each search result. You will see your keyword text highlighted in each summary. Look for modifiers at the beginning or end of that keyword. For example, you may see terms such as "how to find" at the beginning of many of your keyword searches.

"You can get the initial LSI keywords from Google autosuggest and related searches below the search page of your query," writes

Ankit Singla from Blogger Tips Tricks. "The second method would be to get some useful LSI keywords from the Google Keyword Planner or GKP."

Google Keyword Planner is a tool in AdWords that helps you select keywords to target in your pay-per-click advertising. It is set up to help you find LSI keywords for your advertising, but many people use it to find LSI keywords for their content. The good news is that you don't have to pay for advertising in order to use the tool. It's free.

So, while there is mad science behind LSI technology, you thankfully don't have to learn it. Let Google take care of the suggestions for you, or you can rely on a LSI keyword generator to do it.

How to Incorporate LSI Into Your Content

Again, I know this book is about backlinks and not on-site optimization, but it is important to understand how to use them so you will know how to incorporate them into your backlink strategy.

When you get ready to write an article and you have a focus keyword, search for it in Google and identify the LSI keywords. Identify at least two that you can also use along with your main keyword.

Now it's all about keyword density (I cringe when I talk about keyword density). I typically like to use a keyword approximately two to three times in a 500-600 word article. So, in order to incorporate the LSI keywords, I will use my first keyword approximately six times (bear with me on this). Once I finish the article, I will replace at least half of my main keywords with the secondary keywords I located in my Google search.

Here is what it looks like:

- Write an article using a focus keyword approximately six times (or one per 100 words if your article is longer).
- When copyediting the article, replace 50% of those keywords with LSI keywords.
- The result is an article with the focus keyword and a LSI keyword included three times, depending on the length of the article.

It may sound confusing, but you are basically keeping your keyword density low so as not to be flagged for keyword stuffing. Instead of removing your extra use of your keyword phrase, you are substituting it with LSI keywords. Hope that makes sense.

Earlier I said that "keyword density" makes me cringe. In fact, I find the term deplorable. You need to understand there is no correct formula for keyword density. What I am using here is only an example, so you need to determine your own comfort level for how many times you want to use a keyword or LSI variations.

I also want to point out that Google has been able to get rid of spun content based on LSI. Many article spinning programs simply replace similar words in order to "fool" Google into believing it is a unique article. Since Google has become a LSI expert, so to speak, spun content can no longer hide its spammy self.

In fact, LSI is actually used to combat spam according to Roko Nastic in an article written for Search Engine Journal. "Latent Semantic Indexing came as a direct reaction to people trying to cheat search engines by cramming meta keyword tags full of hundreds of keywords, meta descriptions full of more keywords, and page content full of nothing more than random keywords and no subject-related material or worthwhile content."

Are LSI Keywords the Same as Secondary Keywords?

Yes and no. Secondary keywords are additional keywords you choose to use in an article. For instance, if you are focusing on the keyword "affordable SEO," you may also want a secondary keyword of "SEO strategy."

The main difference here is your secondary keywords are chosen by you based on what you want your article to rank for. LSI keywords are chosen based on what Google feels is important to your main keyword.

You are obviously using secondary keywords as you are incorporating more than one; however, the ones you are using are chosen for you by Google. Since Google controls how your content displays in search results, you will be a step ahead using LSI than you would just picking out random secondary keywords.

When you get good at on-site optimization is when you use multiple keywords and then incorporate LSI keywords for each secondary keyword. Confused yet? Okay, let's move on.

LSI Keywords and Your Backlink Strategy

Wow. That was an amazing story we just went through (a little humor for those who decided to skip to the end of this chapter). Okay, fun time is over.

To use LSI keywords in your backlink strategy, you must incorporate what you learn about link diversity. It is important to vary your anchor text on incoming links. Using the same anchor text, especially exact-match anchor text, is a sure sign to Google that your links are not occurring naturally.

Now, knowing what you now know about LSI keywords, one of the best ways to accomplish link diversity is to use LSI keywords as your anchor text. For example, when linking back to your website, don't just link from the term "affordable SEO." Also link from as many LSI keywords as you can.

"Anchor text is a perfect place for you to use your LSI keywords," writes SEOPressor.com. "Instead of anchoring your main keyword, anchoring a LSI keyword tends to make an anchor text much more believable."

Using LSI keywords as alternative anchor text is one of the best ways to accomplish anchor text diversity while still linking from relevant terms. Keep in mind that Google already recognizes these terms as being related to each other so you are ultimately driving traffic while staying out of Google's sandbox.

Don't try to manipulate Google using the same anchor text. Again, you will see how to vary anchor text later, but keep in mind for now that it is something you MUST do if you want the full SEO benefit from your link acquisition activities.

Final Thoughts on Anchor Text

Have you heard me mention link diversity yet? Yes, that was a joke. That is the theme of this entire book, and something all webmasters must practice. Incorporating it into your anchor text variations is a great way to help increase your search rankings while avoiding a penalty.

You should also note that using multiple links in a page is helpful to the reader, but Google generally only reads the anchor text from the first URL and discounts the second. This means that you should use the anchor text you want to rank for as the first link in the article. The second anchor text will probably not be considered for ranking.

The question you have been asking yourself while reading this is "what is the right percentage of each anchor text to use?" Simple question, but there is no right answer for this. If there was, you would see everyone using the same formula, then Google releasing an update to punish those for doing it (as it is unnatural). The goal here is to obtain quality backlinks and let the percentages work themselves out, while keeping an eye on your profile to ensure one isn't too prominent over the others.

Okay. So, on to link diversity? I thought you'd never ask.

5 - LINK DIVERSITY

Part of my work with brands includes helping them build a link profile. This includes internal links within their blog and landing pages as well as backlinks from other websites.

Throughout the years, there have been many changes to the methods SEOs recommend for building links. This can be a problem for webmasters who build up quality links, only to find out they need to change their methods going forward.

"If I had to choose just one thing that our most successful clients have in common, it would be link diversity." – Search Engine Land

"Google wants to see, in a link profile, anchors that display diversity in the form of branded anchor texts." – Neil Patel, Quick Sprout

"Getting links from a diverse group of domains is extremely

important for SEO." - Brian Dean, Backlinko

"Anchor text diversity and link relevancy may be two key factors of Penguin, according to more early analysis." Search Engine Watch

So how do you combat the changes with backlink methods and stay in line with Google best-practices? Link diversity is the solution. Building a diverse link profile can help you withstand algorithm changes and help you consistently rank higher in search results.

What Is Link Diversity?

A diverse backlink profile means that you have backlinks that are varied across different platforms (blogs, news sites, social media, etc.), using varied anchor text (long-tail, exact match, branded, etc.), to different locations (homepage, landing pages, blog posts, etc.), and so on ...

Diverse link building is something that many of the best SEOs and authoritative SEO publications preach.

Well, all four of the above sites are consistently ranked on the first page for search terms related to SEO and backlinks. That should be proof enough that they are doing something right and their methods should at least be considered by others.

So, Why Link Diversity?

Google isn't stupid, and neither is its algorithm. If you build links for one specific anchor, be prepared to be penalized. It can see this trend and will know that you are artificially building your rank.

The same thing goes for when a new website has a ton of high domain authority backlinks. So, you mean to tell me a brand new website, all of a sudden, is being covered by Forbes, Entrepreneur, and the Huffington Post, yet they have little, if any, backlinks to lower domain blogs? Why would major publications be talking about you if no one else is?

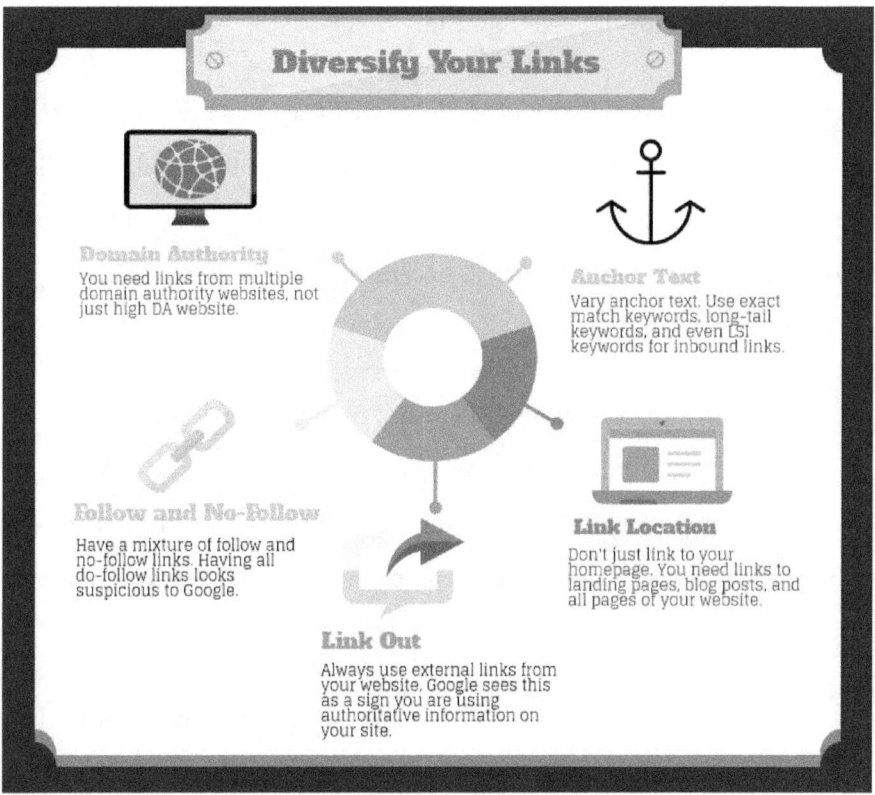

A diverse link profile shows that links are being built naturally.

Websites do not collaborate to link to your site with the same anchor text. Google knows this. However, you will see websites linking back to you from various anchor texts. This is natural and what you want in your link profile.

No-Follow Links in Your Link Profile

I know, most SEOs say that no-follow links are worthless. However, this is a false statement and a few of us believe there is a hidden power with no-follow links. While no-follow links do not "technically" help with ranking, I have a theory that you still need to consider. Again, Google isn't stupid.

Search engines still see no-follow links but they are told not to consider them. This means that Google can see your profile of follow versus no-follow links. If you are building only do-follow links, this makes your backlink profile look unnatural and could lead to problems with ranking.

So, while a no-follow link will not "directly" attribute to your search rankings, it will (in my opinion) affect it "indirectly." Again, Google is going to wonder why you have all do-follow and are absent of no-follow links. Using no-follow links should absolutely be part of your diverse link building strategy.

On a side note, no-follow links can also help you with more than just ranking. I receive quite a few leads from no-follow links. They are still clickable links and lead people to your website which can lead to conversion. It also leads to more visitors to your site which also helps with things such as your Alexa ranking.

Link Location is Important

Vary your link location in order to create link diversity. By this I mean you need to obtain backlinks from numerous different domains and also link to various locations of your website.

Don't simply try to link to your homepage. Most websites won't link to your homepage anyway, as links, according to Google, need to have value. Your homepage is likely your sales page and only has promotional content.

That is why it is important to start and maintain a blog for your site. These articles, if they contain valuable content, will be more appealing to people who want to link to your site. Mix up links to your homepage, blog, and other landing pages.

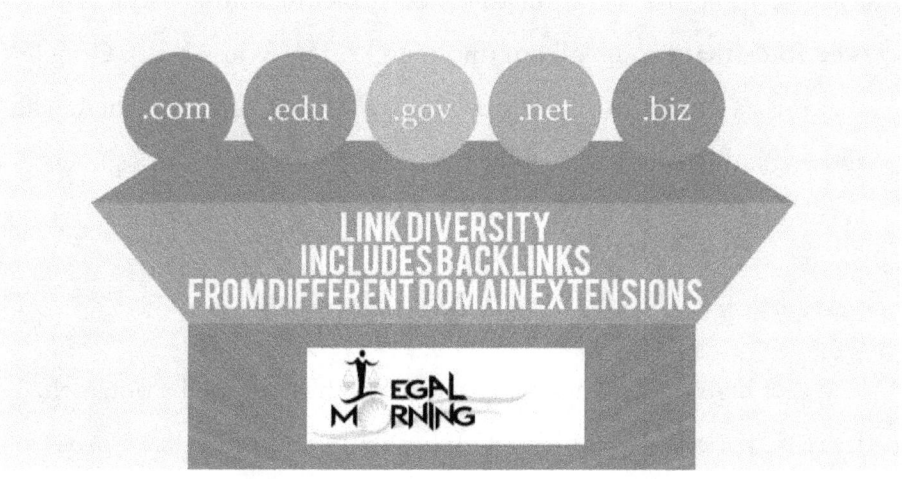

When making a list of websites you plan to pitch, make sure to be diverse by choosing varied domains. Include .com, .net, .biz, .org, and .edu on your list. Simply attaching one domain extension will again make it look like you are artificially building links.

Choose websites of various domain authorities. Don't simply make it a goal to get backlinks from DA50+ websites. I like to set a goal of getting one DA50- site for every DA50+ site.

Vary Your Anchor Text

Everyone has the money keyword they want to rank for. They shoot to link from it every chance they get. This will help you rank quickly but the sustainability is not good and your rank is likely to shift with every algorithm change Google releases. So what do you do?

Don't abandon your money keywords. Anchor text is still extremely important for rank. However, mix in a variation of LSI Keywords that you link from (more on LSI keywords later). Google sees this as similar to your money keywords and linking to them will show link diversity and also help you rank for multiple and similar keywords.

High Domain Authority Backlinks

Get high domain authority backlinks through media outreach. Increase your search ranking with backlinks from sites like Forbes,

Entrepreneur, Huffington Post and more.

Using long-tail keywords is also recommended. For instance, let's assume I am creating a backlink profile for a post about link diversity. I can use "diverse link profile" as my anchor text for some locations and can also use other anchors such as "guide to diverse link profile" or "how to obtain link diversity."

Link Diversity and Google Penalty

Let's pretend that although you have a diverse backlink profile, you still wind up getting a Google penalty. Unlikely to happen if you employ Google best practices but let's assume it's happened for the sake of this example. How can link diversity help you?

When you get sandboxed, the quickest way to recover is to undo what got you there in the first place. Let's assume that your penalty is a result of too many backlinks to your homepage. If you have a diverse link profile, this should only be a small percentage of your links. You will be able to correct the issue without losing the majority of your backlinks, while at the same time maintaining all the hard work you put in to get you those links.

Of course, you don't even want to think about getting penalized and you shouldn't, as long as you don't engage in black-hat techniques, but anything is possible.

Summing Up Link Diversity

At this point, I am sure you get it. Spread the wealth when it comes to backlinks. Don't use the same anchor text and choose sites from multiple domain extensions and of various domain authority. Loading your links to your homepage is a sure sign to Google that you are trying to manipulate search results and you will likely be penalized for it.

6 – LINK WHEELS AND LINK FARMS

So, you need to know about link wheels. You may have been shopping around a marketplace prone to black-hat SEO marketers promising to make your site reach #1. In this chapter you will find out what they actually are and if you should implement them into your link building strategy.

Right off the bat I want to point out that this is not another blurb about black-hat SEO techniques on how to manipulate search results. If you are looking to do so, the actual term you need to search for is "link farm" as this is a completely different topic. I don't teach anything related to black-hat techniques, only methods to help you rank higher and sustain rankings.

Before we go any further, let me answer the first question I am sure you all want to ask:

Are link wheels still effective?

Let's just say I wouldn't be writing about them if they weren't. But, here are a few things you need to keep in mind when reading through this chapter:

- Link wheels are not a magic formula to get you unlimited traffic.

- Some link wheel methods are considered black-hat and will actually do you more harm than good.

- Do not use link wheels as your sole method for trying to increase your search ranking.

- Most link building strategies wind up forming some type of link wheel, regardless if you try to or not.

- Don't confuse link wheels with link farms. Link farms used as part of a link wheel can get you penalized.

- If building a link wheel solely for the purpose of manipulating search results, it will be considered a link scheme by Google.

Let's take a closer look at how to build a link wheel to increase your search rankings.

What is a Link Wheel?

A link wheel is nothing more than linking together various articles back and forth so they point to each other as well as to the property (the website) you are trying to rank. When you visualize the links to all the articles, it looks like the spokes of a wheel with the main website (the one you are trying to rank higher), in the middle of the wheel.

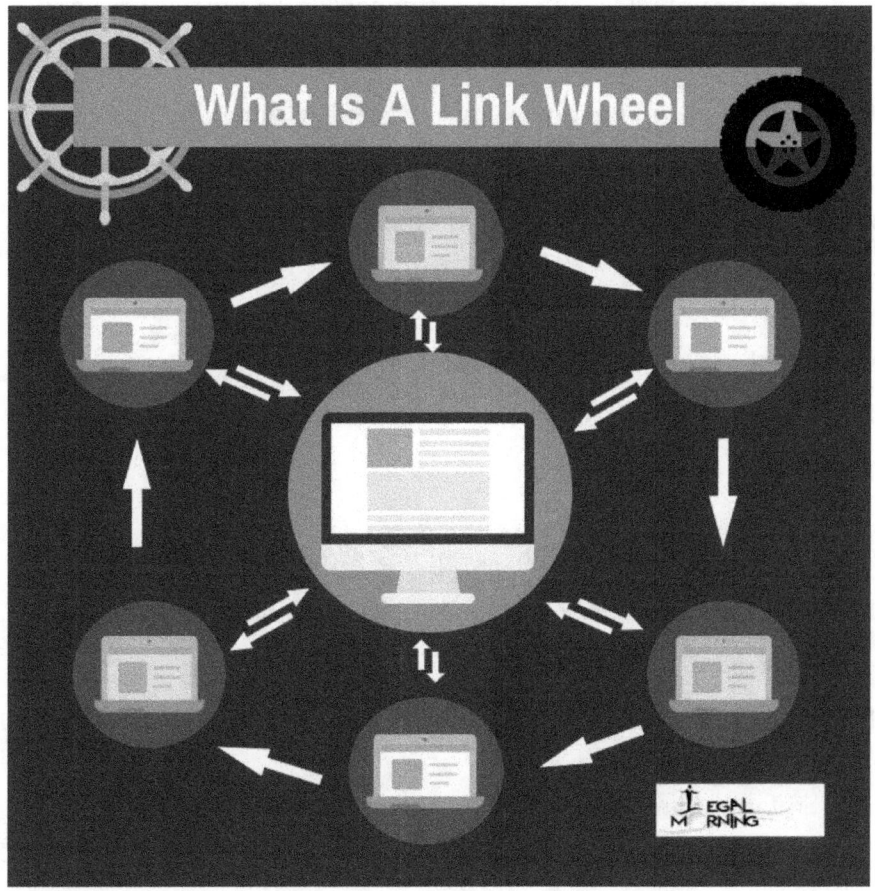

It may sound complicated, but it really isn't. By the time you finish reading this chapter, you will know everything you need to know about link wheels and be able to determine if you should incorporate them into your link acquisition strategy.

Again, remember that a link wheel is different from a link farm, something I will discuss a little later here.

How to Build a Link Wheel

In order to build a link wheel, you need to have what I refer to as your "anchor content." This is the article that you want to benefit from the wheel and the one you want people visiting the most. The majority of the time this is content on your own website, but it could be something off-site depending on the aim of your link building strategy.

For the purpose of this example, let's use an article on Legalmorning.com as our anchor content. We will call this article "AC."

Next, we will need to engage in link acquisition in order to get backlinks to that article. Through our link building strategy, we obtain links to AC from *The Huffington Post* and *Entrepreneur*. These are both high-quality backlinks from renowned sites.

So far our link strategy does not incorporate a link wheel. We are simply acquiring links to our anchor content. Business as usual. Now we are going to incorporate our link wheel strategy.

Our link acquisition will continue as normal. However, we will start to acquire links for our link wheel. Let's say we obtain links from *Forbes*, and *Inc.com*. Our goal is to not only acquire a link to our content "AC," but also to the first two articles in *The Huffington Post* and *Entrepreneur*.

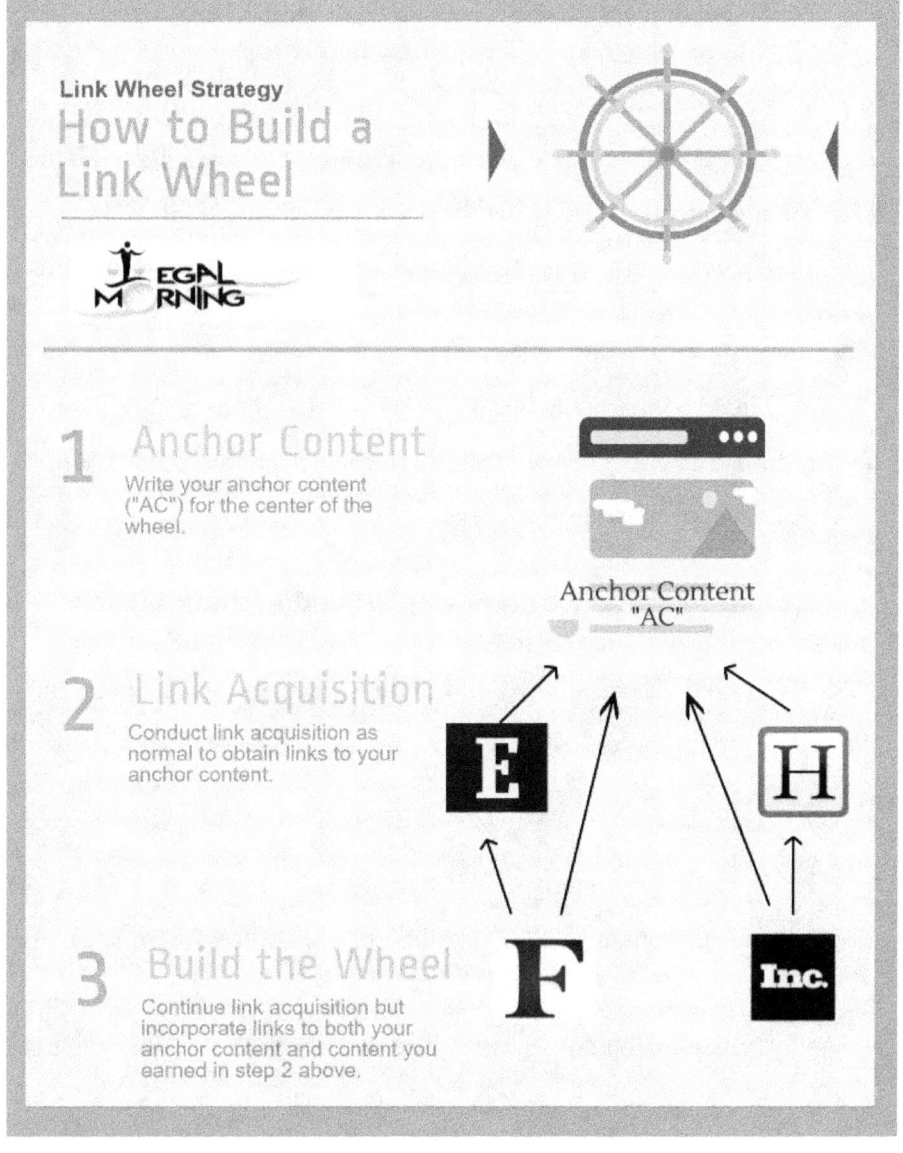

Want an easy way to remember the process? Here is what I tell people – conduct your normal link acquisition, but try to get the publication to link to other high-quality articles that contain links to the same property.

On a final note, do NOT use link wheel software or hire someone to do this for you. Link wheel software and those who offer the service are likely using black-hat methods. They will link together low-quality websites set up specifically for the purpose of tricking Google. You may rank high rather quickly, then drop out of search results completely once Google flags and penalizes your site.

You need to manually build link wheels for them to be effective. If you do use an SEO service, ask them their thoughts on link wheels to ensure they are doing it properly.

You Are Probably Unknowingly Building Link Wheels

As I stated earlier, many link building strategies wind up creating some type of link wheel regardless if they intend to or not. What do I mean by this?

Have you ever posted an article for SEO purposes that links both to your website as well as another article you wrote on the same topic? Does that article link to your website as well? There you go. It's a link wheel. Albeit a primitive one, but a link wheel nonetheless.

Even if you are not building link wheels with your content, there is a chance they are being built naturally by others. Here is an example:

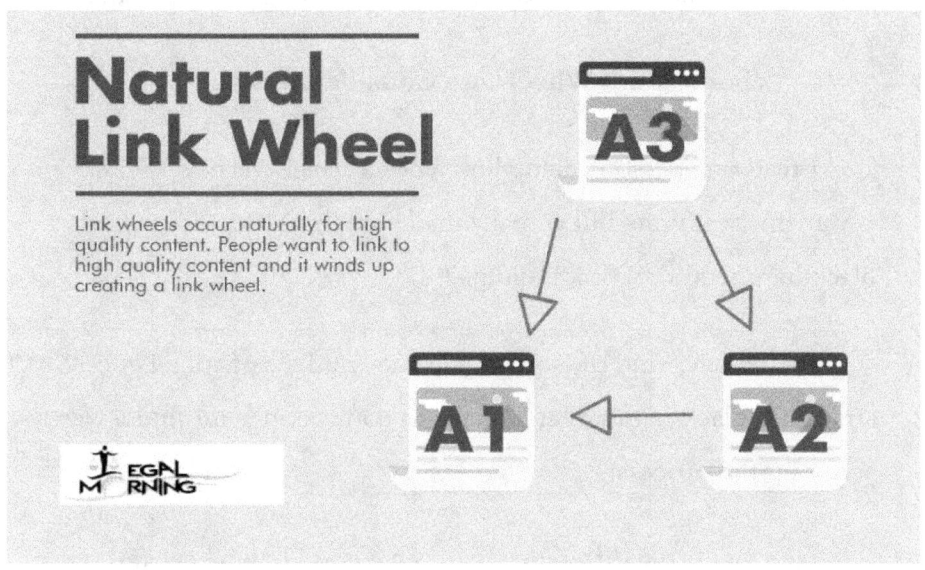

Let's say you have a great piece of content (we'll call it Article 1 or A1). Someone from another site liked it so much they decided to write additional information on the topic and link to A1 (we'll call this piece A2). Now, a third publication comes along and loves information from both pieces and includes a link to A1 and A2 in a third piece (we'll call this A3).

The example above does not show a full link wheel, but it does show the spoke of one starting to form. If the content is of high quality and more people decide to link to it, a natural link wheel will start to form.

Keep this in mind when deciding if you should use a link wheel strategy. If you already are, that is fine, but you also need to understand what makes a link wheel "black-hat" in order to ensure your methods do not fall into that category and get you penalized.

Some Link Wheels are Considered Black-Hat

I read one person calling link wheels "snake oil SEO." The comment was funny but actually made me think. Are link wheels a black-hat method of link building?

Absolutely, kind of, sort of (clear as mud). As with all good SEO strategies, black-hat marketers have to come along and find a way to screw up the process.

So, what is the difference between a good link wheel and one that would be considered black-hat?

Black-hat methods include creating sites on free platforms such as Wordpress.com and Blogger.com (content farms and link farms). They will then write one article (the "money article") that they'll use in the link wheel. Then they'll abandon the blog or fill it up with crappy spun content that no-one cares about.

Here is why it doesn't work.

When you create a blog and no one visits it, you will not have a high domain authority. When you have little or no domain authority, you do not have powerful links. So, while you may have many links within a link wheel, they are useless when it comes to search rankings.

One good link from a high domain authority site is better than 100 crappy links in a link wheel. If you hired someone to create a link wheel for you, make sure you know the sites they are including. If they are using free blogs or directories, you may as well flush your money down the toilet.

Link Wheel Versus Link Farm

One of the easiest ways to make your link wheel a black-hat technique is by turning it into a link farm. When searching for additional information on link wheels, you will probably come across articles that call them link farms. But, they are NOT the same and should be treated as separate link building methods.

A link farm is a group of websites set up for the sole purpose of trying to rank content. Linking to and from the same sites is what makes link wheels black-hat. When you read articles that talk about how link wheels are no longer effective, this is why; it's because they confuse the two.

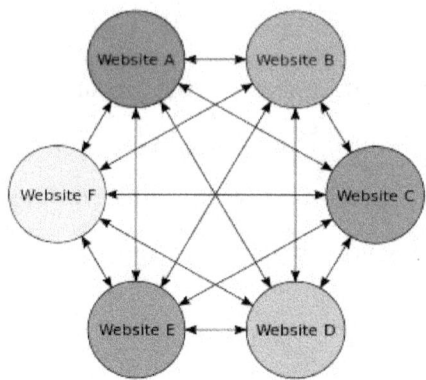

The image above depicts a classic link farm. You will notice it looks similar to a link wheel. The difference? Link diversity and content quality. (Image courtesy of Wikimedia Commons)

You can tell from the image above that a link wheel and link farm look identical. You can overlay them and not see a difference. So, how do they differ?

A link farm uses low-quality websites that you create for the sole purpose of fooling Google. Link wheels are a method of linking high-quality articles that benefit one another. Basically, the wheel may look the same on paper, but it all comes down to the quality of the website you are linking to and purpose for which you are linking.

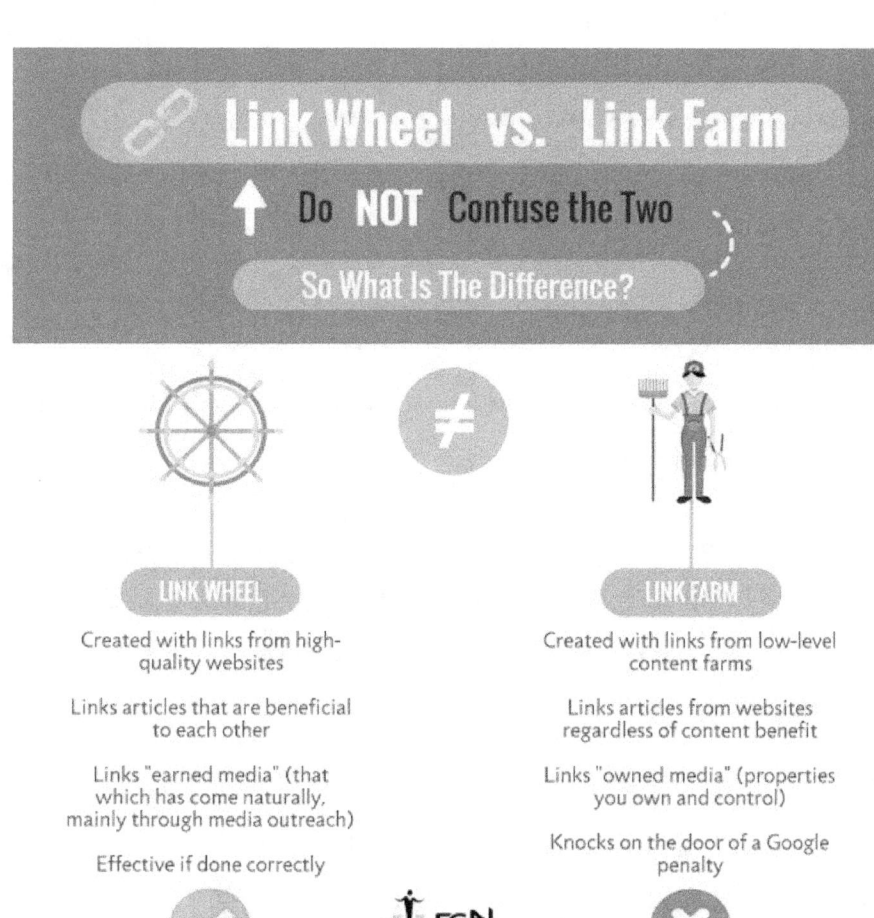

Link farms are created with owned media, properties which you own and control. Black-hat marketers use free website platforms such as Blogger and WordPress to create websites for the sole purpose of linking. They are often from the same IP address as they are hosted on the same server which is a sure sign to Google that you are creating a link farm.

Link wheels are created with earned media, that which comes

naturally as a result of creating quality content. This often involves linking articles written about you as a result of your media outreach plan. It is done to add value to the content being written and not for the sole purpose of rank (although rank is the benefit).

How to Make Your Link Wheel Strategy Work

As stated above, using low domain authority blogs will not work. In fact, it could wind up getting you penalized.

So, how do you incorporate it into your link building strategy without it being considered black-hat? When using link wheels (and frankly all link acquisition strategies), it comes down to link diversity and link quality.

If you put together everything herein, you can logically conclude what will work and what will get you penalized. Here are some tips you can take away.

First, do not use link farms in your link wheel. People who use link farms in their link building strategy are not only wasting their time but are going down the road to a Google penalty.

Your goal is NOT to increase the ranking of low-quality content. Your goal is to increase the ranking of high-quality content. As such, using a link farm in your link wheel is only going to make the house of cards fall when one of the sites gets penalized.

Uniqueness is also key. Do not create identical link wheels

(which is what you would be doing with using link farms). Link high-quality articles to other high-quality articles. For instance, if you acquire a link from *Entrepreneur* for your website, hopefully, that same article can include a link to another high-quality article about you (let's say in *Forbes* or *Inc.com* – maybe both).

Trying to add a link to a low-quality article about you is not going to work and is likely to get you noticed by Google (and not in a good way).

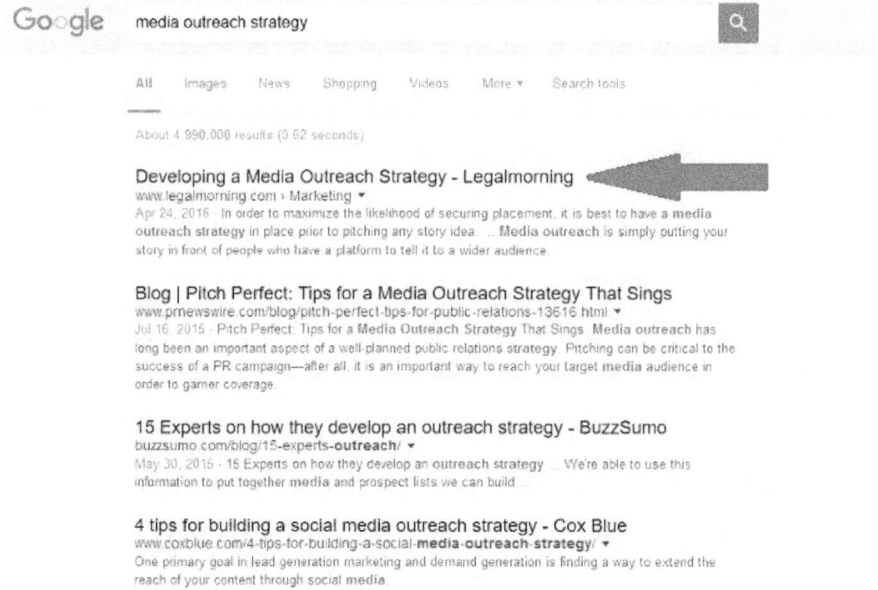

It is better to use a link that already ranks high. You can see above that Legalmorning.com came up #1 for the query of "media outreach strategy." Not only should I use this in my link wheel, but others are already using it in their content (as it ranks high), which is building natural link wheels without any prompt from me.

I also recommend only linking to newer and high-ranking content. After all, people writing articles are likely to use the information that shows up on the first page of search results. Content that ranks higher is likely higher quality or it would not rank so high in search results.

Google knows this as well, since they are ultimately making the decision on where sites rank. It makes your link acquisition look suspicious since you are using content from page 12 of search results (which is two years old) as opposed to something that shows up in the top of results. So, keep building on your newer and higher ranking content and avoid using older, lower ranking links in your link wheel.

Final Thoughts on Link Wheels

When it comes to link wheels, you should incorporate them into your link building strategy. However, don't get too consumed with making sure things are perfect. Do not overcomplicate things and if you are only able to link a few of your articles together, that is better than nothing.

Make sure to incorporate high-quality websites as opposed to directories or free blog sites. Doing so will help you stay on good terms with Google and out of the dreaded sandbox. If anything, keep in mind that link wheels are often built naturally or unknowingly when you engage in link acquisition. Your understanding of how they work will help with your link building strategy and hopefully keep you from having to toe the line of a Google penalty.

Long story short, interlink if it is relevant to do so and not being done for the sole purpose of manipulating search results. Others are doing it for you already and it makes sense to do it if it provides quality to content being written.

7 - CONTENT FIRST, BACKLINKS SECOND

Yes, I know. This book is about backlinks, not content. So why I am covering content? Quite simply, it is because many website owners take SEO out of order. They contact me wanting to increase their backlink profile, yet they have absolutely nothing on their website worth linking to. It would be like riding your bicycle to the Mercedes dealer and asking them to work on the engine.

You simply cannot acquire backlinks to your website until you have the content people can link to. It's the "cart before the horse" concept. Creating quality content that can be used as your cornerstone content is something you need to tackle before any attempt is made at backlink acquisition.

You will find plenty of articles online that talk about the importance of having high-quality content on your site. Without it, there is no way in hell you can build a quality backlink profile. If people do not seem to want to link to you, this is likely why.

Why People Link to You

You are well beyond the black-hat methods of building as many links as you can to your website. As we have discussed in length, you can no longer link to sales pages from exact match anchor text. Not only will this get you penalized, but it defeats the purpose of a link. People want quality information that answers a question, not a page that tries to sell them something before doing so.

You need to be objective when looking at your website. Ask yourself why people would link to you. Is it the graphics? Is it because you paid them? Is it just because? Let me help you with the answers.

The only reason people are going to link to you is because you have something valuable to share. This could be a guide, tutorial, practical advice, the answer to a question, opinion about a topic, etc. The list goes on and on, but as long as you have something that people want to know, you will increase the chances of people wanting to link to you.

Think about this. If you pitch someone asking them to link to your site, yet you don't have anything to link to, that would be like a bald person walking into a barber shop asking for a cut. Don't waste your time with link acquisition until you have something people will link to.

Basically, if it is something you would link to, then hopefully others will too. So can you simply spruce up landing pages or should you have a blog? I get this question all the time; my answer is simple – both.

People Hate Sales Pages

You need to have a blog on your website in addition to well-written landing pages. In addition, your landing pages need to contain answers to questions people will be asking. If it is simply a page to get sales, then it really isn't worth linking to.

The main reason people don't like sales pages is that they hate "being sold to." They want to feel like it's their decision to make a purchase, not something they are being forced into. As such, landing pages should contain the information they want to know such as the answers to commonly asked questions.

This doesn't mean you can't use your landing pages to sell. Hell, that's what they are there for, but make sure to have the customer in mind first. Then, have your call to action and sale pitches placed in a manner that converts without beating people into submission. It's a hard balance to find but doing some A/B testing will get you where you need to be.

As far as a blog is concerned, this is the best place to share your expertise on a topic. This is the most linkable content of your website. Some webmasters actually refuse to link to anything but blog posts (and only high-quality blog posts). So, if only for linking purposes, you must have a blog.

Pages Rank, Not Websites

This is my favorite thing to tell people when they want to create links to their homepage in an attempt to rank their website. Quite simply, it is a fallacy that many still don't understand. The creator of one of the most used SEO plugins for WordPress agrees:

"What most people don't realize is that they're asking the wrong question," writes Yoast in a blog post. "You see, sites don't rank: pages rank. If you want to rank for a keyword, you'll need to determine which page is going to be the page ranking for that keyword."

Being that Yoast is an authority on rank, I tend to listen to what they have to say. In fact, I found the assertion of pages ranking to be true. My SEO strategy for Legalmorning.com does NOT involve acquiring links to my homepage. I actually create high-quality blog posts and then acquire the links to them. I then use internal links from my blog posts to landing pages where I convert most of my clients.

Even though I don't attempt to acquire homepage links, my homepage still ranks high for specific keywords. I actually end up with a double benefit by concentrating on high-quality blog content and internal links as opposed to sending everyone to my homepage.

Now on to some advice on creating quality content that people want to link to. This is only a sampling of the many ways to generate quality content, but these are some of the most prominent methods that case studies have shown help you rank.

Building Content – The Skyscraper Technique

When it comes to ranking content, find out what content is already ranking. I am talking about your competitor's content. Search keywords you want to rank for and find out what consistently lands in the top three spots. Now create content using that framework, but make it even better. This is referred to as the Skyscraper Technique and is very powerful when it comes to content marketing.

The term was coined by Brian Dean from Backlinko. He found that using the framework of content that already ranked high was a better starting point than just pulling content writing ideas out of nowhere.

Note that this is not stealing content. You are not going to rewrite content or plagiarize in any way. You simply want to look at length, keywords, sentence structure, call to action, and more. Here is a real life example.

I decided I wanted to rank for the term "guest post pitch rejection" (and a few LSI keywords that I won't bore you with here). When searching the terms, I found the highest ranking content and found that it only had around 500-600 words. Despite being well-written, there were very few visuals and practically no examples. Here is what I did.

I created a new blog post entitled "7 Ways To Get Your Guest Post Pitch Rejected." Here are some examples of what I incorporated to make it "better." Many of these will be talked about more in-depth later in this chapter, but you can get a general idea of how things were made "better."

The headline was the opposite of what people are actually looking for. People want to know how to get "accepted" not "rejected." We know that negative headlines get more clicks than others so already I created a headline that would generate more clicks. Basically, I made the headline stand out from the same old boring "happy feel good" headlines.

I used long-form content. The posts that ranked high for this keyword ranged in word count from 461 words to 619 words. My post? 1,671 words.

The page that ranked #1 in search results had two images. One was a stock image and the other was a banner ad that had nothing to do with the content. I used six custom-made images and wish I'd used more. Visuals make it easier for people to understand the content and more likely to stay on the page until the end.

I added quotable tweets to the page and Pinterest buttons so people could easily share the content. The more people like it, the more they want to share. The easier it is for them to share, the more likely they will. The more likely … hell, you know the rest.

I used as many real-world examples in the post as I could (like I am doing here). People get sick of hearing you talk about how good something is. They want to see it in action and know the results.

So what were the results? Within three months I was moving between #1 and #2 in search results. Not bad for brand new content published from a lower-domain authority website than the others who also ranked high.

In addition to the increase in search rankings, I accomplished my ultimate goal which was more clients. I have received a steady stream of inquiries from people who want to engage in link acquisition through guest posting. They don't have the time to reach out to various websites they want authorship to. I am able to help them craft an outreach email to use as well as take care of the outreach for them.

One of the funny things is that at the time I am writing this book (about seven months after posting that article); I see another website that just made it to the first page. Guess what method they used? You guessed it. But thanks to link acquisition, I don't have to worry about them taking me out just yet.

What is great about the Skyscraper Technique is that it really does work and is simple to do. You basically make good content better. Now, in order to be effective using this technique, you need to incorporate some of the next methods I will discuss.

Long-Form Content

There is still a debate among SEO professionals regarding how long your content must be. The talking point is ad nauseam and goes like this:

"People have short attention spans so you need to keep your content short" – **FALSE**

If the content is well-written and contains information people want to know, you will keep their attention. In fact, people who read a shorter post that does not answer their questions completely will likely go right back to Google and search for more. You don't want them to go to Google; you want them to stay on your site. So why not give them all the information they need and let them pick and choose what to read? This is exactly why you want to use long-form content.

With that in mind, long-form is all about layout. You need to keep paragraphs short (2 to 3 sentences max) and use call-out sentences such as "here is an example" or "let's see how it works." These type of call outs let people know an example is coming up. You will need to use H2 and H3 headings so that people know which sections answer the exact questions they have.

With long-form content, it is also important to use images and videos. Writing 2,000 words with no breaks will lead to a high bounce rate. However, breaking the content up with relevant images and videos keeps readers engaged.

I also want to point out that long-form content is not just about the length. Some people try to stuff the content in order to increase word count. This defeats the purpose as the content is no longer quality. The point here is that you must use more in-depth analysis for a topic which ultimately increases your word count, not the other way around.

Long-form content is a great cornerstone as it ranks naturally for specific keywords you include in the content. People are not going to link to your content because it is long. They are going to link to it because it is in-depth and authoritative. I will discuss that more in the next section.

Finally, there is a case for shorter content and I agree that using it in certain circumstances is appropriate. But, we are talking about ranking here. When it comes to rank, long-form content has been proven to be the best.

Guides and Case Studies

Guides and case studies can be some of the most linkable content you have on your website. First, they will fall into the category of long-form content which will naturally increase the search ranking. People will also want to link to them as they have specific actionable advice and statistics to back up what is being discussed.

Most guides and case studies fall into the "authoritative content" category. People like to link to research and in-depth information so creating it for them puts you in position to acquire backlinks. Beyond SEO, there are additional benefits as well.

"Case studies are a great way to tell the world how valuable your products or services are," writes Kissmetrics in an article about creating case studies (which incidentally is written in long-form content style). "They go beyond simple testimonials by showing real-life examples of how you were able to satisfy your customers' needs and help them accomplish their goals. With great case studies, you will be able to highlight your successes in a way that will make your ideal potential customer *become* your customer."

Infographics and Backlinks

At one time infographics took over the SEO industry. Everyone wanted to create and post infographics hoping that people would naturally link to them. This was a great technique but became useless once people started saturating the internet with crappy infographics.

Just like written content, no one wants to link to an infographic unless it contains useful information. Websites stopped linking to them so much as they were being used as a purse SEO technique without providing valuable content. So while they have become harder to attract links, they are still viable for a number of reasons.

First, if you create an interesting infographic, people will link, regardless of what the rest of the industry is doing. In addition, you can repurpose the infographic for other areas of your website. Here is what I like to do.

As an example, I will take an article I wrote about earned, owned and paid media. Prior to writing the article, I came up with an outline of information I wanted to cover. I then used this outline to come up with an infographic. Most people stop there and just try to acquire backlinks to the infographic. Where is the value for the linking website? There is none.

I took the infographic and split it up into a series of images and used them in the main article. So, I created an infographic as a value bonus for anyone who wanted to use it, but the article itself is the main content people want to link to. Some use the infographic, some use the article. I get backlinks both ways.

In the next chapter, I will go over a method known as guestographics which is one of the best outreach methods to get backlinks to your infographics.

Summing it Up About Content

I could write an entire book on content. Actually, I think I will. But, in the meantime, I don't want to waste any more time with it here. However, I wanted to give you a foundation for it so that you can put yourself in a better situation for acquiring backlinks (almost there, next chapter).

You need to remember that you must have content people want to link to. Stop expecting people to link to your homepage or sales pages and stop expecting Google to rank those pages just because you want them to. Start creating quality blog content so that people will want to link to you.

8 – LINK BUILDING STRATEGIES

I once had a client ask me what the Skyscraper technique was and if I used it for content. What was meant to be a test to see if I knew anything about SEO, turned out to be a lesson I am going to give you today. That lesson? Test your SEO provider to make sure they know what they are doing.

You need to ask these questions of your SEO firm. If they are unable to answer, then you are throwing your money away. They may have different names for the methods you read about, but they should still be familiar with each one. Why should they know all these techniques?

Well, let's just say I didn't invent any of these methods. These are all techniques used by some of the best SEO minds in the world. They are techniques that are tried and true and I can testify they work. If your SEO provider is worth a damn, they should know most (if not all) the techniques I am about to talk about. This is because you can read about these techniques all over the internet. I would expect them to know these if they are really good at what they do and are applying best practices in order to help you rank higher in the search results.

Another lesson I want to provide you with is that you must always read and keep up to date. Digital marketing in all its forms changes on a regular basis. Link acquisition is no different. New and better methods are being talked about in white papers and case studies that you need to know about. Sign up for email alerts from publications such as Search Engine Journal or Kissmetrics.

The more you read, the more you know. The more you know, the better off your website will be. Even if you do not apply these methods yourself, you will at least learn new questions to ask your SEO provider to make sure they are keeping up with the latest and greatest methods for link acquisition.

With that in mind, I am going to list all of the backlink acquisition techniques that have been shown to work. These are all white-hat methods of link building and have the most success. Some of them are more work than others, but after trying them all you will find the few that work best for you.

Blogger Outreach

Blogger outreach is something you need to get used to. Many of the methods I cover herein require you to contact webmasters and writers in an attempt to acquire links to your website. Just about every backlink acquisition method involves some form of blogger outreach.

Blogger outreach is nothing more than making contact with a property where you have identified a backlink opportunity. You will need to let them know what you have to offer and the value they will receive. Targeted blogger outreach will be covered in individual sections herein, but there is also a "cold blogger outreach" method that you can do without using any other link acquisition method.

A cold blogger outreach is simply contacting a blog owner, presenting your content, and asking them to link to it. It is still a viable backlink strategy, but it doesn't yield you as many backlinks as the other methods I am about to talk about. It can also be one of the most time consuming methods out there.

"One of the least sexy ways to build links is through email outreach," writes Neil Patel. "It sucks because it's time consuming and boring, but it works. *It actually works really well.* For every 100 emails you send out, at least 5 of them should be linking back to you."

Here is a sample cold outreach email:

Dear [name of site owner],

I was reading your blog XYZ and really enjoyed your article on

media outreach.

I have an in-depth guide about media outreach that you and your readers may find useful (Insert Link). Please feel free to use it in any of your content."

[Your Name Here]

There is a debate if you should ask for a backlink at this point (e.g., "if you decide to use the content, I would really appreciate attributing it back to my site with a link"). Regardless, you can see what cold outreach is, as opposed to some of the more targeting outreach we will detail later.

This method still works, but don't be disappointed if your success rate is not that high.

On a side note, I use a version of the above outreach template to start building relationships for Collaboration Outreach (a method I will cover more in depth later in this chapter). Basically, I send the same email but only include the first sentence. I tell them I was reading their site and tell them about an article I really enjoyed. If they strike up a conversation, a relationship is building which can be beneficial later on.

Guest Posting for Backlinks

Before we go any further, let me say this as loud as I can – "Guest posting is NOT dead." Okay, let me explain.

In 2014, a bomb was dropped on the SEO community. Then head of Google's spam team, Matt Cutts, posted an article on his blog titled, "The decay and fall of guest blogging for SEO." The SEO community proclaimed that guest posting was officially dead.

I don't want to take away from Matt Cutts, but too many people hung on his words like he was a god. They took everything literally and failed to find the true meaning in his blog post. What Cutts was saying is that using guest posting simply for backlinks is no longer a viable option.

Cutts was talking about spammy articles created solely for the purpose of tricking Google. Years ago people would generate keyword stuffed articles with exact match anchor text and offer these to webmasters in exchange for a link. This is the type of guest posting that Cutts was referring to.

"Guest blogging is not in itself a method of gaining guest blogs," writes Neil Patel in an article about link building posted on Search Engine Land. "If a website owner or editor trusts you to create high-quality content, they are not giving you permission to start aiming backlinks at your website. They are instead trusting you to produce excellent content that their readers will love. If you have a byline or an occasion to mention some *other* articles you've written, then you may be entitled to a link."

Guest posting is still, and probably always will be, a viable option for generating backlinks. Most webmasters only allow a link from your author profile which is still a link. So the way you need to approach this is to become a contributor on websites that allow a backlink in your profile. You then need to generate high-quality content that is useful to that website. While you are not technically exchanging an article for link, it does have the same connotation which is why I suggest only doing this with high-domain-authority websites.

So how can you get an opportunity to guest post on a high-domain-authority website? Well, you must incorporate blogger outreach. As opposed to cold blogger outreach, you are actually offering a website value – quality content.

To increase your chances of being accepted to guest post, you must nail your pitch. This takes a little time to perfect, but I cover the process a little more in-depth in a separate chapter at the end of this book. Make sure to pay close attention to what goes into your pitch or you will be wasting your time with this method.

Guestographic Backlinks

I wanted to cover guestographics next as they are very similar to guest posting and also incorporate blogger outreach. The only difference is you are using an infographic as added value. This is yet another method developed and phrase coined by Brian Dean.

Dean's philosophy with guestographics is simple:

Great Content + Targeted Outreach + Added Value = Links

For guestographics, you are offering great content (the infographic) by using targeted outreach (blogger outreach). So what is the added value? That's right, guest posting. Instead of simply offering a webmaster an infographic, you are going to offer them some original content.

Most infographic outreach is cold and begs people to share your content. This means the webmaster has to actually do some work in order to help you. So how does it help them? With guestographics, you offer to write a blog post to accompany the image, which adds more value to the website.

This also gets you away from a potential Google penalty. Google hates embedded links such as those within infographics. When you provide a guest post along with the infographic, you are simply using the infographic as an image and getting a contextual link from the body of the article. Good news is if the infographic is ever deleted the article with link will likely remain.

Here is how the outreach email reads. I am not going to re-invent the wheel so this is the approximate wording provided by Dean in his case study on guestographics. You will need to customize this to fit the site you are pitching and the infographic you want linked to.

Hi [enter name here],

I was on the hunt for some advanced on-page SEO tips today and found [enter article name here].

I really like that you emphasize the importance of on-page SEO (it's easy to overlook with all the info about links and social signals!).

Actually, I just put together an infographic about advanced on-page SEO.

As someone who writes about on-page SEO quite a bit I thought you may get a kick out of it ☺

Let me know if you want to check it out.

Cheers,
Brian

Once a reply is received, you offer the value to the site owner. Simply provide them with the link to the infographic and then offer to provide a unique guest post to accompany it. Here is where I differ slightly from the Dean method.

Dean recommends a 250-300 word blog post. While that is great, I recommend writing a full post of at least 600-800 words. Why? Let's say in the future infographics become so unpopular that people begin to remove them from their websites. If that happens to be the case (call me paranoid), you will still have a blog post with a link.

Guestographics has become a preferred method for infographic outreach. In fact, some websites have even adopted it as part of their guest posting conditions. An example is Business2Community whose contributor guidelines require that all infographics submitted be accompanied by a minimum of 300 words of original content that talks about the infographic. Again, I vary from Dean slightly and recommend writing a full blog post in accordance to the site's regular guest post guidelines.

Another tip is to offer to supply a blog post when you pitch the infographic with your initial outreach – if your pitch is accepted. "As someone who gets about five of these infographic pitches daily I can say I'm more likely to reply to the ones who offer to follow up with the unique content to go with it in the first place, rather than me having to ask them for it." says Sian Phillips from Tweak Your Biz.

Collaboration Outreach

I am always looking to collaborate with other writers. By collaborating, I am always reaching out and asking writers if they are working on anything that I can assist them with. The good news for me is that I have a ton of clients and can hook them up with industry experts in just about every field known to man. I have built many relationships this way and it has wound up getting me backlinks that I never asked for.

It can be tempting when collaborating with others to ask for a backlink. Do not do this. You should also never exchange links or pay for links which can also be tempting. What you are doing here is similar to corporate social responsibility.

You are helping other writers out of the good of your heart. In return, they will remember you and likely link to your content when they are writing. There is no metric to see the success or failure of this method, but it continues to work for me.

I have also turned this into a soft-close method for my media outreach clients. I use the contacts I have built to be able to reach out and see if any writer is interested in talking about anyone I represent. Placements come easier and in more publications which makes my clients very happy.

Linking to Other Properties

One surefire way to get backlinks is to link to other websites. However, you can't just link to a website and watch the backlinks roll in. You actually need to conduct some blogger outreach.

If you find a good blog worth linking to and decide to do it, make sure to reach out to that blog once your article goes live. Tell them you found their content worth linking to and provide them with a link to what you have written. Many times you will find them linking to the content from their website just to show others where they have been mentioned.

One way to increase your chances of this earning links is to link to properties that document all of their mentions. If a blog has a "news" section, see if they link to all of the blogs that mention them by name. Once you link to them and notify them, you will likely see a link to the article on your website.

Think about it for a second. Can you imagine how many backlinks I am going to generate to the electronic version of this book? Every person I linked to has been notified I used their content as a reference. I invite you to check the metrics as you will see the results of this method using the book that taught you this in the first place.

A little caution about this method though. If this is the only method of link acquisition you are using, it could likely cause issues for you. To Google, your link profile will appear to be a link-exchange scheme (you are linking to a website in return for a link to your website). That is why you need to adhere to link diversity principles in your plan as well as applying this method.

Broken and Dead Backlinks

Want to get a ton of links from high-quality websites in a hurry? The broken and dead link method is the way to go. Broken and dead links are slightly different, but the process is the same.

Dead links are links that lead to nowhere. Either the target website is out of business or the page on the website no longer exists. Broken links are links that go to an actual website, but the URL is not entered correctly. This is normally the fault of the webmaster who didn't properly check to make sure the link worked.

For the purpose of this book, I lumped both of them together. You simply need to adjust your outreach email to match if you are trying to replace a broken link or a dead link.

Start by looking for competitors in your niche that have gone out of business. Think about it. A website spends quite a bit of time building quality backlinks. Once they cease to exist, all of the links going to that website are now no longer active.

Simply go to Google and search for terms such as "bankruptcy" or "out of business" isolated with terms relevant to your industry. Here is an example of how I was able to help a client.

A few years back, Brand.com filed for bankruptcy and ceased operation of its website. There were thousands of backlinks leading into the website which had become irrelevant. These were backlinks from authoritative websites with high-domain authorities. My client worked in the reputation management industry which was a perfect fit based on the content on their website.

The client performed their own link acquisition and simply used me to create cornerstone content for their website. What I did was isolate a list of backlinks to Brand.com using Ahrefs and then sold the list to the client. It was a win-win for both of us and the client was sending emails for weeks and acquiring backlinks easier than any other form of link building they had been doing.

So why would a website be willing to change the link to yours? Well, make sure they know that a broken link can actually harm their website. If they have links leading to dead ends Google will see this and potentially rank it lower as it links to nothing as opposed to authoritative content. You are helping them out and claiming a benefit in the process.

If you are not lucky enough to find a large website that just went out of business, you will need to manually look for links. There are many websites such as Ahrefs and Moz that can do this for you, but let's look at a free way you can do on your own.

First, you will need to use Google Chrome. I know, I know. I don't like it either, but I use it simply because of the extensions that are available which brings me to the next step. You will need to install an extension called *Check My Links*. Once installed, you will see the icon on your toolbar on the right-hand side.

Next, perform a Google search for the term related to your backlink. You will have to isolate the search to find all pages related to your term that also contain backlinks. Simply search for that term in Google to get a list of pages which contain that keyword phrase (hint – try using LSI keyword variations as well).

Once Google returns your results, simply click on each page that you feel is relevant and then click on the Check My Links tab at the top right. The extension will check the entire page and notify you of any links that lead to nothing (either broken or dead). Check out the context of the anchor text.

Finally, if the context and anchor text are relevant to the content you have on your website, reach out and offer it up as a replacement.

You can repeat this process using the search term "[Keyword]" + inurl:resources.

This will find websites with resource pages that you can also check. Resource pages are great as they link to numerous sources, many of which are no longer live. Since they want to make sure they link to the most relevant resources, you will find success using this method.

So now that you have your list of websites you want to contact, what is the best wording to use? Here are some examples of outreach emails you can use to help get your backlink. Of course you will need to tweak it based on your actual search results and the website you are reaching out to.

This one comes from Moz.com and is specific to replacing broken backlinks on resource pages.

Hey [name of author or website owner],

I was looking through your suggested links on [website name] and noticed a few broken links.

Let me know how to reach the webmaster and I can send a list their way!

Also, if you're open to suggestions, I think [name of your website or specific article] would be a great fit.

All the Best,
[Your Name]

    Here is a great one from Art of Emails that is tailored specifically to broken links within articles or other content (slightly modified to make it more of a template for your use).

Hey [name of author or website owner],

I was looking for a few resources on momentum trading and I came across your very informative guide: [Title]

I noticed that one of the resources you mentioned on [topic of broken link here] no longer exists.

I recently created an extensively researched guide on [topic]: [Link]

[Talk about some of the highlights and value from your link –

be specific about what is talked about in your link as it applies to the article you want linked from].

It might make a good addition to your article.

Either way, keep up your insightful articles – Google sure loves those 10,000+ word tomes.

Signoff

As with any template, you will need to make slight modifications. I also recommend personalizing as much as possible to make yourself stand out from other emails received by the webmaster. You can find plenty of other template examples by going to Google and typing in "broken link outreach email."

Now, if you are finding broken backlinks but the context is not fitting to the link you want to replace it with, here is how you can still get a backlink (hopefully). Simply mix in the "collaboration outreach" strategy and notify owners there is a broken link. Here is how you do it.

Send your outreach email and list the link that is broken. Send them the correct link or another link that would be suitable. Since your link won't fit the broken one, this seems like you are not getting a benefit. That is true initially. However, if the webmaster appreciates you helping them out and sees that your email is not self-serving, this could lead to an opportunity to collaborate.

Final thought on broken and dead backlinks. You will find articles that talk about how to do this method on Wikipedia in order to gain a link from the site. I recommend staying clear of Wikipedia for numerous reasons I cover more in depth later in this book.

Adding Yourself to Resource Pages

Now that you know how to find broken links on resource pages, use it to find pages that have NO links to a resource you have. You can use a quick email to recommend your guide, eBook, or even website as a source. Here is what I am talking about.

Do a general search for a website that has a resource page for a specific keyword. For example, let's say you want to offer the webmaster a guide you put together on the "linking from LSI keywords." The first thing you want to do is perform the search using the following parameters:

"lsi keywords" + inurl:resources

Of course you can change your search term to things like "guide to backlinks" or anything you feel will return results that will give you an opportunity.

Google will return the resource pages of all blogs using this term. You simply go to the page and find out if they have anything that talks about linking from LSI keywords. If not, contact the webmaster and find out if they would like to use your guide. You can use any of the many outreach templates herein, customized to fit the request.

I like to combine this method with the broken backlink method. Resource pages can be quite large which means there are a ton of links and they become outdated quicker than others which should provide you with more link opportunities. Just make sure you send the correct outreach email.

Links That Have Moved

Take advantage of your competitor rebranding by gobbling up any links they leave behind. This is similar to the broken and dead backlink method, but the actual link is not broken. It is there, but now at a different URL.

Let's say a company rebrands from "Legalmorning.com" to "MikeIsCool.com" (I wish). If the site does not create a proper redirect, the link will lead to nowhere. This is where you step in.

Reach out to the webmaster and point out that the link no longer leads to the URL. Offer them your link in return. For this, you can use the same templates as the broken and dead backlink method, just customize it to fit your need.

You can find these sites by keeping up with news in your industry. Another way to do it is through a Google search. Make sure to use "Google News" as you want to find press releases with rebranding announcements. Use this parameter:

"[topic or industry]" + rebrand

Here are some additional search terms you can use, courtesy of ArtDriver:

"Rebranded as" + Niche Specific KW

"Announcing our new website" + Niche Specific KW

"Service no longer available" + Niche Specific KW

"This page is no longer being updated" + Niche Specific KW

"Citation Needed" + Niche Specific KW

"Dead Link" + Niche Specific KW

Acquiring Backlinks from Mentions

If you are worth anything in the industry you operate, chances are people are already mentioning and linking to you. However, sometimes you get mentioned and the webmaster will fail to link to your site. There could be a specific reason why they chose not to, but you need to reach out and see if they would be willing to add it anyway.

So how do you find these links? If you are using programs such as Ahrefs or BuzzSumo, they are automatically checking for you. You can set your preferences to receiving emails of these brand mentions which you can then check to ensure there is a backlink.

If you don't want to pay for this service, you can do it for free manually. First, search for websites that mention you by name but don't link to you from your brand name. Here are a few search queries put together by Powered by Search in a blog post on turning brand mentions into links.

- **General Search Query:** "client name" -site:client.com
- **Blog Posts Mentions:** "client name" -site:client.com -site:yelp.com blog OR post
- **Partnerships, Testimonials, About Us:** "client name" -site:client.com -site:yelp.com about OR testimonial OR partnership

This will return a list of Google results that you can then search manually to see if there is an actual link or not. For those that do not have a link, reach out and ask for it.

If the search results are not accurate due to the client name being too generic (e.g., such as my name – Mike Wood), Powered by Search recommends placing modifiers specific for your industry like these for a dentist and orthodontist.

- "client's name" **+dentist** -site:client.com
- "client's name" **+orthodontist** -site:client.com

Now comes the fun part of blogger outreach. You need to contact each one and request your link. Here is a sample outreach email for you to use. This originally appeared on Ahrefs, a site I highly recommend for you to use in order to find all your brand mentions.

Subject: You forgot to link to [brand name / page] in your article/post/page about [topic]

Body: Hi [Webmaster],

I was just going through [post], and saw that you've mentioned [your site] in it. It's great to see our site featured on a great site like yours and I was just wondering if you just forgot linking out to our site in addition to mentioning it? I think you did, because a link would be appropriate at that place and would just allow your visitors to visit our site without having to make additional Googling.

Either way, have a great day and all the best for [their site]!

Regards,
[Your Name]

Want to take this one up a notch? Simply add in the link building technique of broken backlinks. Instead, find brand mentions of competitors who have gone out of business. You can amend the previous outreach email to state something like, "I wanted to let you know that XYZ is no longer in business. If you are interested, I offer a similar article that contains similar information which would be useful to your readers." I think you see the point here.

Allowing Guest Posting on Your Blog

This one is debated by webmasters. There are many out there who recommend NOT allowing guest posts on your website. This is because of the amount of spam people try to force down your throat. It is risky to accept guest posts, especially if you do not understand editing (removing spam links, etc.). However, I think most SEO professionals would agree that there is a benefit to accepting guest posts.

When you accept guest posts, you are increasing the likelihood of obtaining backlinks to your website. This is because those who submit content to you are more likely to link to it. Here are a few examples.

I advertise ghostwriting services on my website. In order to show people my writing quality (my writing quality is also debatable), I link to guest posts I have previously written. These sites are getting backlinks simply by allowing me to submit content to their site.

Another thing to keep in mind is that people are more likely to link to content they have written. When I write a post for a publication such as Entrepreneur or AllBusiness, I will link to other content I have written on websites such as Content Marketing Institute or Tweak Your Biz. CMI and TYB get backlinks for allowing me to guest post as I link to the content from places like Entrepreneur and AllBusiness. Hope that makes sense.

Now, allowing guest posts is not as easy as it sounds. You need to make sure you have the proper guidelines set up so contributors know what to expect. You also need to update your website terms so people understand that the opinions in the guest posts do not necessarily reflect your own. So, while this is a good method to get backlinks, it is a little more complicated that it sounds and shouldn't be your first choice for acquiring links.

9 – WIKIPEDIA BACKLINKS

Wikipedia is my bread and butter. Although I am an online marketer and offer a variety of services, Wikipedia is the majority of my business. I want to qualify myself before I go further as I hope you heard my advice on Wikipedia backlinks. You will find many articles out there talking about the benefits of Wikipedia backlinks, but trust me – **DON'T DO IT!**

It's not worth your time and you would get a better SEO benefit from acquiring backlinks from a few high-domain authority websites. The reward simply isn't worth the cost.

Over the years, Wikipedia has become a minefield for marketers, often causing more trouble than it's worth. However, Wikipedia is still effective and can be used by content marketers to both assist with SEO and contribute to the mission of the world's largest encyclopedia.

Content marketers often misunderstand how backlinks work in

Wikipedia. They think that if the topic is relevant, simply adding a link to the "external link" section of a page is good enough. Not so.

Adding a link to Wikipedia is like surgery – if not done correctly it can cause many issues, including having your added domain listed as spam and banned from Wikipedia.

It is so difficult to obtain and maintain a Wikipedia link that I ceased offering this service a long time ago. However, knowing that many marketers are going to do it anyway, I wanted to share some best practices on Wikipedia backlinks. If done correctly, it can still be a great benefit to your SEO.

Wikipedia Moves from Do-Follow to No-Follow

First, let's look at how backlinks have changed in Wikipedia over the years. When Wikipedia launched in 2001, backlinks were all "do-follow" – created for SEO purposes. With Google's heavy weighting of Wikipedia and its backlinks, marketers were quick to pick up on the SEO effect.

Wikipedia editors quickly caught on that spam was aplenty. The community took massive steps to help curb spam, including changing links to "no-follow," which have less SEO effect, and creating a blacklist to block domains they considered spam.

"No matter where you place it, Article Page, Talk Page, User Page, Project Page, whatever, no Link will get any credit at the major search engines." This according to Carsten Cumbrowski, writing for

Search Engine Journal.

Cumbrowski continues, "This will not eliminate SPAM at Wikipedia, but it will over time certainly reduce it a bit. Especially the spam of invisible pages that have virtually no traffic but at least some PageRank is now virtually a waste of time for any spammer."

Now, even though no-follow backlinks have less effect on SEO than do-follow backlinks, Wikipedia backlinks are still some of the most coveted in the marketing industry. This is because Google gives heavy weight to Wikipedia links despite the fact that they're no-follow.

Where Should You Link?

I will share what really works in securing Wikipedia backlinks, based on my professional experience.

Do not simply look for citation-needed entries. Wikipedia automatically searches for and scrutinizes completed citation-needed templates. If the added links do not contribute to the entry's quality, they will be removed and potentially blacklisted.

Find entries in dire need of cleanup and expansion. In these cases, you have a better opportunity to contribute quality content – expanding the knowledge shared on that topic and contributing to Wikipedia's goal of freely sharing knowledge.

To find an article needing more quality information, go to the all-articles-to-be-expanded page. More than 1,800 articles appeared in this category in one month this fall. Explore more than one month for an endless supply of pages that could benefit from your input.

Knowing the Types of Links

Now that you know where to find places for your links, let's look at the best-suited types of links.

Make sure the links come from a reliable source. Wikipedia's rules on reliable sources are lengthy. Basically, don't use self-published sources (press releases, etc.) and make sure that the linked website employs fact-checkers to ensure accuracy of content.

Check whether Wikipedia already considers the source as reliable. See if the cited website has its own article. For instance, AdAge has its own Wikipedia page, which increases the likelihood that links from its site will be accepted as a reliable source.

See if your cited website has been used as a backlink. Go to the search box and type in the URL that you want to check. A site that has been used numerous times also increases the chances of it being accepted as a reliable source.

In this screenshot, you can see that AdAge has been used 301 times as a reference in Wikipedia. You also can see the top result is AdAge's own Wikipedia page.

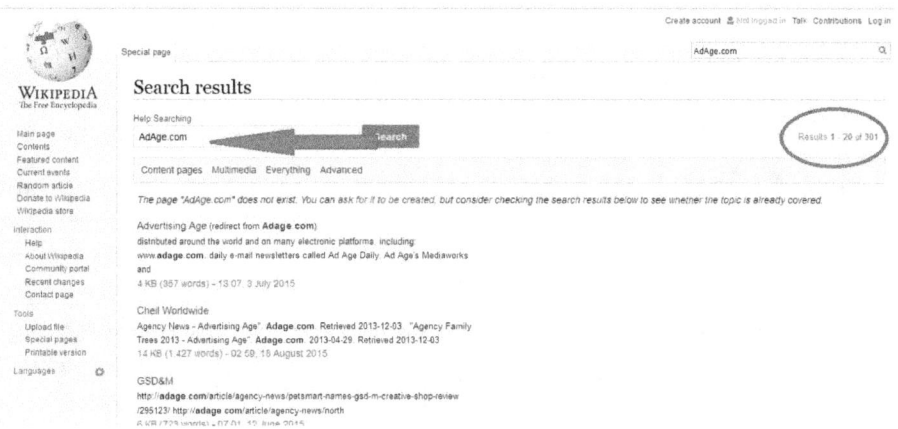

Make sure the link is more than a landing page. A link to a landing page without information to support the content is considered spam by Wikipedia editors.

Link directly to the relevant content page. The link must have content that supports the information you are adding. For instance, if you are adding information about advertising, you cannot simply link to your website's home page as the authoritative source.

You must connect to the exact page that supports the content, similar to how you would cite sources in a research paper or industry study.

Putting it Together

Now it's time to add the link. To do things correctly, you must contribute to the encyclopedia – adding more links than just the backlink you want to include. Here is an example of how it works:

Let's say you want to add a link from The Motley Fool to the Big King sandwich article on Wikipedia. The link relates to the advertising of the Big King in 2014 – that section is empty in the entry. Adding the link not only enables you to place the link you want but it also contributes positively to Wikipedia.

You also have a *USA Today* citation about advertising of the Big King – although you're not looking to secure a backlink to USA Today, incorporating it adds credibility to the entry.

Now, you must write the content for the entry that is supported by the citations:

"In 2014, Burger King reintroduced the Big King as direct competition to McDonald's Big Mac. (USA Today citation) Part of its advertising campaign was that the beef used on the sandwich was bigger than that of the Big Mac. (The Motley Fool citation)"

By incorporating two credible sources into the added information, you increase the chances that your intended link (The Motley Fool) will survive scrutiny. I also suggest adding even more content to the entry to truly enhance the value of your contribution.

Follow the proper format to add links. I go in-depth into how to do this with a three-step guide for adding citations which can be found on my blog. Make sure to know what you are doing – adding a link incorrectly can lead to an editor accusing you of spamming even when you aren't.

Summing Up Wikipedia Backlinks

In conclusion, I cannot reiterate it enough – do not simply link from Wikipedia for the sake of linking. Make sure to do it correctly and contribute along the way. Introducing content that adds quality to the encyclopedia is likely to help your link last a long time and greatly benefit your SEO efforts. Remember that there is NEVER a guarantee with Wikipedia so any process you employ is not foolproof, just a best practice.

BONUS - NAIL YOUR GUEST POST PITCH

Earlier in this book I discussed guest posting as a viable way to get backlinks to your website. As with all of these methods, you should strive to find the easiest most effective way to do so.

When you start to pitch websites to guest post, you will have a high rate of rejection (actually you will have a huge "no response" rate). You will also be competing with many others who are asking for the same thing, the opportunity to write for the same website. So how can you increase your chances of guest posting?

When it comes to getting accepted to write for a website, first impressions are the key. You must be able to nail your pitch. There are many others submitting pitches to the same website so you want to stand out from the others. I discussed the following article earlier in this book, but included a modified version from its original form for you to read here.

Keep in mind that most of your rejections for guest posting will be the direct result of your pitch. Get it right and increase your chances of being accepted.

The following article originally appeared on Legalmorning in August 2016.

Oh yes, guest posting. If you want to rank high in search results, guest posting on other websites is a necessary evil. Some people don't like to do it, but guest posting can help you establish your authority in your field and help build high-quality backlinks. The problem? How to make a perfect guest post pitch.

I have written guest posts for numerous websites throughout my career. I have also received a countless number of pitches from people wanting to post on my blog. I have used my experience with both to come up with surefire ways to get rejected while pitching a guest blog post. Wait, what? Yup, I said it!

If you want to get rejected by blogs and websites when pitching them guest post ideas, you will want to make sure to do any or all of the following. These are surefire ways to make sure to have your pitch email deleted or in the spam folder of the webmaster you are contacting.

Not Personalizing Your Pitch

The first thing you need to do when you engage in blogger outreach is to address the editor personally. Don't just address them by name, show them you understand something about them. I receive so many pitches that begin with "Dear Sir or Ma'am" which tells me they know absolutely nothing about me or my blog. I don't even read beyond that introduction as it's not worth my time.

One of the best guest post pitches I received started like this:

"Dear Mike,

Hello from Texas. Hope you're not getting too much snow up there in Indiana."

That introduction catches my attention. I could tell the person sending the email actually took the time to find out more about me (or at least read the "about me" page of my website).

Above anything else you do, a template introduction that does not address the webmaster personally is a great way to get rejected or ignored when requesting to guest post.

Pitching a Site That Doesn't Accept Guest Posts

Unfortunately for the pitch I showed above, I do not accept guest posts on my website. How can you tell? Simply look at my blog. You will not see anything posted by someone other than myself. You will also not find a "contributor guidelines" or "submit guest post" link. This is the first sign that I don't accept guest posts.

When you pitch a site that does not accept guest posts, don't plan on getting a response. Very rarely will a site that does NOT accept guest posts decide to make you their first one.

Just like finding blogs that do NOT accept guest posts, it is easy to find others that do. Again, simply look at the blog and see if multiple people have posted content. Look for guest blogger guidelines or anything that would lead you to believe they would review a guest post pitch. There are also sites that compile lists of websites that accept guest posts.

Pitching to a Dormant Website

In this case, don't plan on your guest post pitch getting rejected, plan on it getting ignored. If the blog you are pitching to is not active, the chances of being accepted are slim to none.

The easiest way to tell if a website is dormant is to look at the blog and find the date of the last post. You can also look at the homepage and see the copyright (most webmasters update the copyright year). These are all indications that the blog is no longer active.

Not Understanding the Blog You Are Pitching

Here goes the most damning sentence you can ever write while pitching a guest blog post.

"I have read your blog and …"

The "and" is usually followed with something like "I would love to submit a guest post about XYZ." The only problem, the "XYZ" they mention has NOTHING to do with the blog niche. As my site is called "Legalmorning," I receive pitches all day long that go like this:

"I love your blog on Legalmorning and was wondering if I could submit a guest post on how to find a criminal lawyer in San Diego."

Guest what? My site has nothing to do with law unless you are looking to market your legal firm. It is obvious the person who "read [my] blog" did no such thing. These emails also go right in the trash bin and blocked so I don't have to deal with their spam in the future.

Here is one of the best examples which comes from a blog post on TINT. The blog is specific to marketing and technology but that didn't stop one spammer who failed to read the niche. After receiving a guest post that started with the classic "I read your blog," the editor asked for some specific topic ideas. Here is what she received:

"Hi Muriel!

I apologize for the late reply! Would you be interested in an article about:

– How to Layer Rugs

– 6 Gorgeous Mid-Century Modern Living Rooms

– Inspiration: Decorating with Air Plants

If you have any alternate topic ideas we would be happy to write about that instead. We are excited for the opportunity to possibly be featured on your website!"

If you are going to write a pitch that doesn't get rejected, you need to make it personal to the website. Here is a great example of how I would send a guest post pitch to myself to guest post on Legalmorning:

"I read your blog and particularly love your article on why people need to use LSI keywords in their content writing. I also think it's important to vary anchor text. I see you currently don't have content that talks about anchor text and was wondering if you would like me to write a guest post that talks about this topic?"

This blogger outreach pitch would tell me that the person read my blog, knows the content I have and don't have, and is pitching me a specific idea and not just a category. Which brings me to my next way to get your guest post pitch rejected.

Pitching a Category and Not a Specific Idea

The last thing a webmaster wants to see from someone pitching a guest blog post is someone saying they will write anything "related to SEO" or that they can submit articles "about content writing." You and everyone else are writing for these categories listed on the blog. Why else would you be pitching them?

So what makes you different from the other 50 emails received pitching the same category? Pitch an actual idea. Instead of saying you can write anything related to SEO, give the webmaster some choice topics. For example:

Topic 1 – "How to Vary Anchor Text for Link Diversity"
Topic 2 – "Why Google Hates Your Backlink Profile"
Topic 3 – "5 SEO Methods to Stop Using Immediately"

When you pitch specific ideas, the person receiving your guest post pitch will know you took the time to look at the blog and review the different stories already published. Hopefully you are pitching some ideas that have not already been covered on the blog as this is a good way to get accepted, instead of rejected.

Giving them three choices also allows them to counter-pitch. I have pitched guest blog posts to websites with three topic ideas, only to have them turn around and give me a 4th or a variation of the first three.

Guess what? I'm not offended as my pitch was not technically rejected and I still get the opportunity to submit a guest post.

Using a Generic Subject Line in Your Email

This should go at the top of this list, because using a generic subject line is a great way to get rejected or even sent to the trash bin without being opened. If you are familiar with email marketing, you know that subject lines are the most important thing. Without a catchy subject line, people will not even open your email.

Why do you think it would be different for blogger outreach?

I am the worst with subject lines but thankfully I have a copy editor. Even if you don't get help from someone, at least be a little more specific than "guest post inquiry" or "request to submit content."

One idea that I see people using quite frequently is using the potential article title as the subject line to their pitch. Personally, I now use something funny or a specific fact about the person I am writing to (e.g., where they live, where they graduated from).

Sending a Guest Post Pitch Contrary to Contributor Guidelines

This is one that has to drive editors crazy. When you send a pitch but do not conform to the guest post pitch guidelines, you are surely going to be rejected. It shows that you don't pay attention to detail and that you failed to take the time to see what the site is about (two things previously covered in this article).

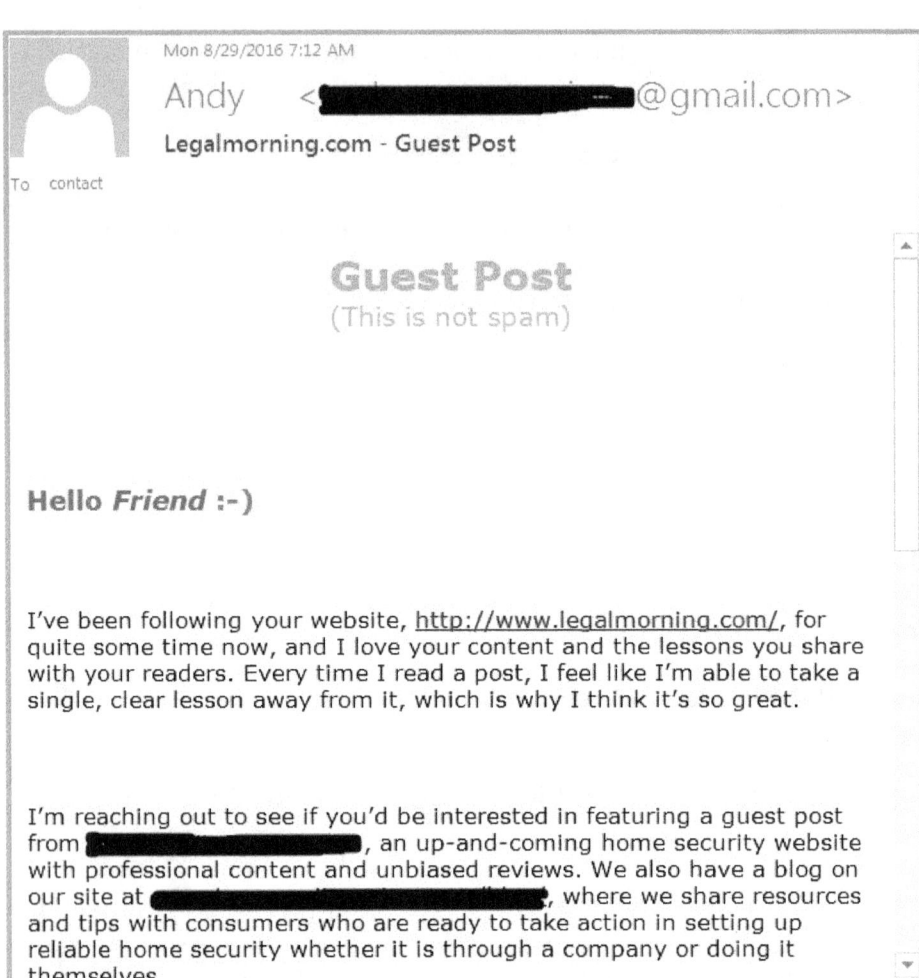

Had to throw this email in. It was received exactly one week after this article originally published on my blog. Unfortunately for Andy, he did all the mistakes that I talk about in this article. Sorry, Andy. Maybe you should have read this first.

If the guidelines say to send them three topic ideas, then do so. Sending an email void of topic ideas will surely get you ignored. If it says use the site contact form, then use the site contact form. Some sites want you to pitch ideas while others want you to submit complete articles. Pay attention to what they want. It's their house so play by their rules.

Final Thought on Guest Post Pitch Rejection

The idea is obviously NOT to fail. If you are doing any of the things listed in this article, you are decreasing your chances of success. As someone who pitches (regularly accepted) guest post ideas, I can swear by the methods I write about. I can also tell you from the experience of receiving blogger outreach pitches which ones go directly in the trash.

BONUS – 50 SHADES OF SEO ADVICE

Okay, so it is a poor play on words. Fact is, I never read the book or saw the movie but it was catchy at 2:00 AM when I was finishing up the formatting and pasting these together.

Backlinks are only one of many aspects of SEO that you need to understand. Content writing, on-site SEO (meta descriptions, etc.), keyword placement, etc. are all part of the bigger picture. As a bonus, I tracked down 50 SEO professionals who were willing to give you a single piece of advice on SEO.

Some are similar which tells you how important they are. Hopefully you will see that some are the same as in this book which tells you I'm not as full of bullshit as my friend thinks (I told you, Shoshan). And yes, I said friend (singular). I don't get much of a life outside of family and writing.

"Write your content for your reader, not for SEO. When your readers are satisfied, Google (and other search engines) will be satisfied and they will reward your site accordingly." – Sue Laurent, NSMarketing

"If you have taken a content marketing strategy and worked on developing evergreen content, you should go back and revisit each piece on a yearly basis. You should examine your headliners, images, article links and call to actions to make sure you originally checked off your SEO checklist. You will also be able to modify the headliner, fix broken links, shrink images to improve load times, add alt tags, change link destinations and many other things that will help you improve upon SEO." – Leonard Kim, InfluenceTree

"Off-page SEO is easy to overlook. Monitor your Page Authority (PA) & Domain Authority (DA) in order to quantify and better manage your off-page strategy." – Rob Sanders, RSO Consulting

"The simplest bit of SEO advice I would give is to install the Yoast plug in and check its comments. Red or green, you can learn from it. Yes, it's not set in stone as something you have to follow to the word, however, if you aren't an SEO professional (not many writers are) then it's a handy starting point to learn from. You can go back and amend your post and see if you then tick the boxes on Yoast." Sian Phillips, Content Editor at Egg Marketing PR

"SEO is a changing game. Long gone are the days you can post crappy content, get random links and still expect to rank. To truly be successful in the long run, focus on writing content that is highly useful to your customers and build links to high authoritative content. Always remember to think of search engines as human beings and make decisions for the long run." – Chirag Kulkarni, LiRX

"A page without images is like a day without sunshine. Or like a book without a cover. Or like oatmeal without packaging." - David Leonhardt, The Happy Guy Marketing

"The thing that I think separates a good link builder from an average one is effort. That's it. You have to be invested, and willing to put time in to build relationships; that's how you build strong links." – Chris Jones, MWI

"Think beyond just keyword phrases and create useful, unique, informative content on "topics of interest" that your prospects will read. Ask and answer their questions in greater detail than your online competition." - Nancy McDonald, Invenio SEO

"If you build it, they will come doesn't apply to your website. Actively promote your content and website through any all mediums. Develop meaningful relationships with other publishers and eventually the links, shares, and traffic will come." – Derek Miller, CopyPress

"Investing time and effort to get your IA right from the outset will save you a lot of time and effort further down the line so I'd strongly recommend anyone who's serious about technical SEO to brush up on how best to optimize a site's structure and master the use of

Google Search Console and Bing Webmaster Tools to ensure the spiders look kindly upon your web properties!" – Luke Fitzgerald, Wolfgang Digital

"The best method to evaluate whether or not a backlink is desirable is to consider the site and page it will be presented on, and their ability to influence a positive action for your business' target audience. If the site link has questionable merit by that standard, its value is limited." - Jordan Brannon, Coalition Tech

"Anchor text is back in a big way. Just keep it varied and natural. Google isn't looking anymore. Penguin is. And Penguin will get you all on its own if you are threading the needle on anchors. And Penguin won't hurt you like a manual penalty. Most experts call it a filter, not a penalty. It will happen over weeks and/or months as opposed to one day." – Tony Newton, Linktub

"With just about every aspect of SEO, from content creation to backlinks, quality is vastly more important than quantity. High quality content gets shared many more times and one authority backlink is worth more than 1000 unrelated links. Essentially, it's like hearing a stock recommendation from Warren Buffet vs 1000 people on the street mentioning the same stock." – Ed Brancheau, Goozleology

"Writing for people is the most important part of optimizing your website for search engines. Without optimizing for people, readers will leave your website causing your ranking to decline. Worse, people will never convert on your page that does rank. Without converting people, ranking in a search engine has no purpose." – Nick Leffler, Your Brand by Nick Leffler

"When writing content, always start by writing for the user first. Your audience--and Google--will appreciate you for it and give it the visibility it deserves." - Raleigh Kung, Burns360

"If you want to get found for a particular service then you need a web page strictly about that service. For example if you are a landscaper and want more patio construction jobs then you need a web page strictly about building patios." – Alex Bungener, Digital+, LLC

"Do things ethically and with quality in mind. If you do, you won't need to scramble after every algorithm update, because you'll already be following the practices search engines want you to follow." - Geoff Hoesch, Dragonfly Digital Marketing

"Having QUALITY well-optimized content is the #1 important ranking factor for SEO Today. Yes, backlinks are still VERY important, but what good is ranking your content if it's not going to convert into a lead or sale for you." - Jeff Lenney, JLenney Marketing, LLC

"Get your NAP right! NAP stands for the Name, Address, and Phone Number as it is listed online for your business. Accurate NAP is critical for businesses wishing to rank well in the local organic search results because search engines like Google take the data into account when determining which companies to show for geo-targeted searches." - Garrett Nann, POP Advertising Partners

"Content is king. Just ask Disney! Developing unique, relevant, educational and intriguing content for your audience will drive your organic search rankings and increase web traffic. Content comes in many forms - video, blog, social media, news releases, images, white papers, case studies, e-books, etc. Create a variety of content consistently over time for your website and you will be rewarded." - Randy Mitchelson, iPartnerMedia

"Twitter is the most powerful outreach tool for getting a hold of writers and webmasters when it comes to link building. Even more important than email." – Chris Weaver, MWI

"Never 'set and forget' even the best links. Proper link management means regularly checking in on your links to make sure they're still complementary, high-quality, and high-authority. There are sites to mass check for dead links and overall link analysis, but nothing compares to manually checking your links at least once per quarter." - Jessica Mehta, MehtaFor

"Put effort into the design of your web pages. Great content is wasted if the UX is not optimized with clean design, proper header tags, media and other on-page formatting (font sizes, lack of clutter, click areas and so on). I'm not going to say it's the top factor (links probably take that crown), but it's crucial as Google robots' #1 goal is to mimic human behavior." - Victor Bilandzic, Motava

"SEO is pointless unless you have a content funnel that moves website visitors from searchers to buyers on their schedule. Use lead magnets like guides, webinars, and whitepapers to have visitors identify themselves and subscribe to your email." – Perryn Olson, Marketing Consultant

"Focus on answering the questions your customers are asking in long-form, strategic blog content. Make sure you are showing them what to do, not just telling them what to do. It's much easier to get backlinks to stellar content!" – Derric Haynie, Vulpine Interactive

"Don't forget your videos! Business websites and social media are continuing to feature more and more video. You can take advantage of keywords in your video by including them in any descriptors of it and also by having a transcript of the video on the site." – Rafael Romis, Weberous Web Design

"When many start their journey with SEO, most jump straight to the point of keywords and finding backlinks. That's cool and all, but for people to maximize their time they should be doing their research first. Looking at the pre-existing competition and understand who the audience is. Building out a campaign only to find out the audience is not your ideal customer is a pain in the butt. Lost time and resources." – Lawrence Tam, Pressure Point Marketing Inc

"It's easy to get carried away with SEO and forget about your audience. Always remember you are writing for your audience first, producing excellent content should be your first priority that means if you rank in search people will be glad they clicked your link and want to read more." - Amanda Webb, Spiderworking

"Write for people, edit for search engines. You have to provide search engines the proper data and content in order to rank. But if no one wants to read the page once they land there, it's pretty useless." - Eugene Farber, BUZZergy Marketing

"Create a good story. If you can tell a good story through content, like an awesome article or entertaining video, and hundreds or thousands of people share it and link to it, then that's going to have a huge impact on SEO. Then do it again 100 times!" – Eric Hebert, Evolvor Media

"If there's one theme I come across pretty much every day, it's people looking for shortcuts to SEO success. They don't exist. Like most things in life, success is often hard won, earned and deserved. This is most definitely the case when it comes to generating business from Google and those who succeed embrace this simple truth." – Dave Robinson, Red Evolution

"SEO is not search engine optimization. SEO is knowing all the correct elements necessary to build a website the right way." - Eric Riter, Digital Neighbor

"Keep it natural. Search engines have evolved over the years and are really developing an understanding of context." – Simon Jones, Miromedia

"Remember that googlebots needs text to see. So always explain your images in unique descriptions to ensure you get indexed for the content you have up." – Kim Ekin, Presence Marketing

"Good SEO is done by traditional link building and on-site optimization. Great SEO is done by producing a heck of a good and shareable content and then using trending channels to promote it." – Johannes Kanter, GettingGrowth

"If you are stuck for content ideas, use Google's autocomplete feature. For example, start typing the beginning of a question then type different keywords or even letters to see how it ends: 'what can I do in a...what can I do in b...what can I do in c...'" – Ahmed Khalifa, IgniteRock

"I always tell my clients to not overthink it when it comes to SEO. The best way to boost your SEO is to use the same wording that people are using in Google, instead of trying to be unique or descriptive. For example, people are more likely to search "branding strategist" instead of "brand coach" simply because more people are used to seeing "branding strategist" online." – Jessica Freeman, Jess Creatives

"Search engines can drop rankings for no apparent reason and are often unpredictable. They can fluctuate on any given day at any time due to changes in search engine algorithms, SEO efforts made by competitors or both. As SEO evolves, the rise and fall of a websites position is simply inevitable." – Chelsey Moter, seoWorks

"SEO is always evolving and shifting, but writing great content and building fast, well designed websites will never fall out of style. Track and understand SEO cycles, but remain focused on creating the best user experience possible. Keep [user experience] as your compass to guide SEO efforts and you'll always find yourself on the right side of the algorithm." – Adam Tanguay, Weebly

"More users are conducting searches on mobile devices than ever before and Google is taking notice. Google has been changing their index and ranking factors to reflect the emphasis on mobile. Ensuring that your site is optimized for mobile is crucial!" – Amanda Hummel, Anvil

"At the end of the day, you need to remember that all the keywords in the world won't matter if you don't have good copywriting. Talk like a human, and tell your story with strategy and heart." – Kelly Mazur, North Palm Digital

"Don't get stuck in your old ways. SEO evolves quickly. Hypothesize, experiment, and discover new methods of helping your organic results improve." – Brandon Maciel, New Dimension Marketing and Research

"In a word: integration. SEO is not a stand-alone discipline, so the best SEO campaigns are integrated into all marketing activities to provide the digital footprints the search engines are looking for. By creating a solidly integrated digital marketing strategy that includes SEO, this prevents companies from chasing the latest algorithm changes or trendy tactics." – Chris Gregory, DAGMAR Marketing

"Winning at SEO will never be as easy as it was yesterday. As tough as the algorithm is now, you'll wish it was "this easy" in another five years. Start today in making even one improvement to your website within Google's guidelines that makes your site more valuable than your competitors' to your target user." – Hannah Nelson, Blue Corona

"A 10-pg site with high quality content will outperform a 100-pg site with low quality content." – Clint Henderson, Wired SEO

"Once link juice if flowing from one root domain extra links from the same site matter less and less. Instead of pursuing the same news and article links always be chasing new site opportunities to get as many unique sites linking to you as possible." – Kevin Pike, Rank Fuse Interactive

"Think of SEO strategy as a 3-layer pyramid. Technical SEO forms the foundation, content optimization fills in the middle layer and authority building (i.e. link building) forms the peak. Like building a house, without a solid foundation, no matter how well you do parts 2 and 3, it will not be as successful. Make sure search engines are not impeded by technical roadblocks and the rest of your strategy will fall nicely into place." – Jon Clark, Fuze SEO, Inc.

"Use your keyword research to inform your content topics, but don't kill your content by over key wording. Readers can sniff spam a mile away." – Alyssa O'Mara, O'Mara Marketing & Media

"Don't stop with keywords or backlinks. SEO is an all-encompassing practice. It includes everything from psychology and design to user experience, creativity, and technology." – Cameron Corniuk, Goldstein Group Communications

"Stop trying to game the system. If you are focusing on how you can stuff, mislabel, or trick the search engines, you are doing it wrong. Try this instead: create honest, frequent content. Play by the rules. The results will speak for themselves." – Emily Carter, 24K Creative

ABOUT THE AUTHOR

Mike Wood is an online marketer, author and Wikipedia expert. He is the founder of Legalmorning.com, an online marketing agency that specializes in content writing, brand management and professional Wikipedia editing. He is a regular contributor to many online publications where he writes about business and marketing. Wood is the host of the Marketing Impact podcast and author of the books *Link Juice* and *Wikipedia As A Marketing Tool*.

www.ingramcontent.com/pod-product-compliance
Lightning Source LLC
Chambersburg PA
CBHW071442180526
45170CB00001B/426